BASIC TRAINING FOR RESIDENTIAL CHILDCARE WORKERS

ABOUT THE AUTHOR

Beverly Boone grew up in Reading, Pennsylvania, and attended
Alvernia University, becoming the first in her family to graduate
from college. She attended The Pennsylvania State University as a
teaching assistant in English and received a master's degree in
Writing. She also became a lecturer in English at the university,
teaching basic english skills to academically disadvantaged students
and developing a curriculum for teaching the transfer writing
course. After leaving Penn State, she moved to San Diego, which
has remained her home. It was here that in 1992 she opened
Milestone House, a residential treatment center for emotionally disturbed teen girls. Ms. Boone is the author of two previous books, *To
Be Somebody* and *The Road Ahead.*

BASIC TRAINING FOR RESIDENTIAL CHILDCARE WORKERS

A Practical Guide for Improving Service to Children

By

BEVERLY BOONE, MA, CGHA

CHARLES C THOMAS • PUBLISHER, LTD.
Springfield • Illinois • U.S.A.

Published and Distributed Throughout the World by

CHARLES C THOMAS • PUBLISHER, LTD.
2600 South First Street
Springfield, Illinois 62704

© 2012 by CHARLES C THOMAS • PUBLISHER, LTD.

ISBN 978-0-398-08708-1 (paper)
ISBN 978-0-398-08709-8 (ebook)

Library of Congress Catalog Card Number: 2011031701

With THOMAS BOOKS *careful attention is given to all details of manufacturing
and design. It is the Publisher's desire to present books that are satisfactory as to their
physical qualities and artistic possibilities and appropriate for their particular use.*
THOMAS BOOKS *will be true to those laws of quality that assure a good name
and good will.*

Printed in the United States of America
MM-R-3

Library of Congress Cataloging-in-Publication Data

Boone, Beverly.
   Basic training for residential childcare workers : a practical guide for
improving service to children / by Beverly Boone.
      p. cm.
   Includes bibliographical references.
   ISBN 978-0-398-08708-1 (pbk.) -- ISBN 978-0-398-08709-8 (ebook)
   1. Child care workers--Training of. I. Title.

HQ778.5.B66 2012
649'6--dc23
                                        2011031701

PREFACE

*B*asic Training for Residential Childcare Workers celebrates the profession of childcare worker in residential care. Many childcare workers (and indeed their supervisors) fail to understand how important their work is. Within these pages, readers will come to recognize not only how integral to best practice the childcare worker is, but also that effectively training childcare workers is key to the success of any residential program.

Milieu therapy is the job of childcare workers. It is the most pervasive therapeutic intervention that occurs in residential care. Sadly, most childcare workers (and their supervisors) know little or nothing about milieu therapy, and as a result, little or no training about milieu therapy takes place. *Basic Training for Residential Childcare Workers* aims to change that by offering a handbook on milieu therapy for both childcare workers and residential care supervisors. After defining milieu therapy, the book examines key elements of milieu therapy: program structure, the house schedule, maintaining good boundaries, setting limits, rewarding positive behavior, and consistency. Because many of the elements of milieu therapy revolve around concepts, each element is carefully explained and examples of actual situations that may occur in the residential setting are included. Clear and specific suggestions for improving childcare practice are included throughout, so childcare workers or supervisors can immediately put lessons learned into actual practice as the need arises.

Since consistency is so important to the success of milieu therapy, effective communication becomes essential to the professional residential childcare workers. This book offers practical suggestions and examples of how childcare workers can improve their communication with coworkers on shift as well as with their supervisors. For many childcare workers, the most intimidating duties are the many written tasks they are required to complete. Each major writing task is discussed in detail, and general instruction on writing is offered to help make all on-the-job writing tasks easier and more confidently done. In addition, childcare workers must know their milieu so that they can remain consistent and resourceful in their interactions with children in care, and special suggestions are offered to increase a childcare worker's familiarity with his or her workplace and to learn to use its resources most effectively. Finally, a consistent worker is a healthy worker. The final chapter of the book discusses ways childcare workers can maintain their own well-being in a profession that can be stressful and sometimes overwhelming.

Each chapter concludes with a detailed chapter review to reinforce ideas and emphasize key points. Also included at the end of each chapter are exercises that are designed to help readers put the material covered in the chapter into actual use and practice. Overall, this book is meant to be user friendly, imparting information that can be readily absorbed, practiced, and implemented by childcare workers and their supervisors, who can use this book for training purposes. Whether you are a childcare worker or a supervisor, *Basic Training for Residential Childcare Workers* is designed to help improve outcomes for children in residential care, increase effectiveness of childcare workers, and reduce stress and burnout for staff.

B.B.

INTRODUCTION

In 1992, I opened Milestone House, a residential treatment center for emotionally disturbed teenaged girls. With very few resources at the time, I relied heavily on the generosity of many members of our local community to get Milestone started and to keep it going through the early years. The first three to five years are difficult for any business, but I think more so for sustaining a group home. The support I got from many generous people was key to Milestone's survival.

When I started Milestone, I had no experience with residential care at all. My background was in education. I had been a lecturer in English at the Pennsylvania State University, where I began to have a special interest in learning disabilities. After moving to San Diego, I continued to work with people of all ages who had learning disabilities. Soon my colleagues and I noticed that I was especially adept at reaching the toughest of teenagers and getting them at the very least interested in learning. Translated, this meant I was assigned the students no one else wanted, but I enjoyed working with those troubled souls because I have always gravitated toward those who need the most help.

About the time of this realization, a friend approached me and asked me if I would consider opening a group home in a house that a friend of his owned. The house had been leased to a boys group home that had lost its license, and now the owner wanted to find someone to put a similar operation into the same location. I did not know what a group home was, but I told my friend that I would think about it. After some research, I found my entrée into the field that would consume my life for the next decades. A high percentage of those in the child welfare system were learning disabled, and many of them did not receive proper diagnosis or school assistance for their learning differences. There was my mission. I called my friend and said that I would love to open a group home at the location.

So began the odyssey of getting the home licensed and approved by our host county. I hired a consultant who was a former licensing analyst in California and got the generous guidance of a busy author and business expert who advised me in all aspects of running a business. It took nearly a year, but soon all the pieces were in place. We had gotten our nonprofit status, submitted a program statement, received our license, and were approved for placements from our host county. On September 29, 1992, Milestone House opened its doors and welcomed its first client. I hired good people to handle the childcare work and social work duties and contracted with strong mental health providers to provide much-needed services.

I set about learning the business and experiencing with our girls the effects of abuse, neglect, and molestation on their psyches. Quickly, I became familiar with the most common psychiatric disorders found in our girls and learned the best treatment modalities under the guidance of professionals who were either working for me or had contracted with us. I read book after book, article after article. Once I got to know the child victims with whom I worked, I was unwaveringly determined not to let them down.

Of course I also focused on my area of strength: education. In a very short time, school districts recognized that I knew my stuff and was not going to rest until appropriate services were provided to any of my girls who needed them. Many a dormant workability program was dusted off and implemented, girls were placed in more or less structured environments according to need, and extracurricular activities were accessed because, of course, children in special education had a right to participate, too. My mainstreamed girls got equal attention as their progress was tracked through regular contact with their teachers. At the first sign of a problem, strategies were put in place to remedy the situation.

The backbone of the Milestone program has always been our dedicated staff of childcare workers. I have always valued our childcare workers and have looked for ways to help them to do their jobs better and reduce burnout. Childcare workers are on the front line of the therapeutic work done at Milestone and any residential treatment program. A facility can have the best social worker, the best program manager, and the best psychologist in the state, but that facility will soon fail if its childcare workers are not well-trained, effectively supervised, and appreciated for the critical work they perform.

As I searched for better ways to support our childcare workers, I recognized that there were several conceptual areas about the job of childcare worker that were difficult to train. Things like having good boundaries, the importance of following the schedule, and the benefits of rewarding good behavior were difficult for managers to adequately convey to new childcare workers in their initial training and thereafter. Furthermore, when these concepts were not adequately communicated to staff, problems resulted both for the childcare workers themselves, who might experience burnout, and for the children in their care, who might actually be detrimentally affected by a childcare worker's unintended mistakes. I vowed that I would one day write a book to help childcare workers and managers to more effectively train and be trained. The result you hold in your hands.

Over the years, we have worked with hundreds of girls and their families, helping them through their difficult teen years and guiding them into adulthood. Many of them are doing very well and remain in touch to update us on how their lives are going. After eighteen years in business, it is humbling to realize how many lives we have affected through our work. Working in residential treatment for children is as rewarding as it is challenging. Childcare workers help some of our society's most deserving victims and help to set them on a path to a productive and fruitful life. It is my hope that this book will assist childcare workers as they approach their profession by offering them tools they can use to more effectively perform the tasks presented on the job as well as to assist them in minimizing stress and avoiding burnout. It is also my hope that my book and books like mine will help to elevate the profession of childcare worker to the level of respect it deserves. Residential care runs not on the work of administrators but on the professionalism of a staff of childcare workers. Childcare workers are and always will be the most important part of residential treatment. Well-trained and well-informed childcare workers are the key to successful residential care.

CONTENTS

BASIC TRAINING FOR RESIDENTIAL CHILDCARE WORKERS

Chapter 1

RESIDENTIAL CHILDCARE WORK: AN INTRODUCTION

The career of providing care for children in residential placement is one that can be rewarding as well as challenging. The work appeals to many because of the opportunity to make a real impact on the day-to-day life of some of our society's most at-risk and disadvantaged youngsters. Experience gained working with this population is invaluable whether a childcare worker chooses to remain in the field or move on to other areas of social services. Because of the importance of childcare work, colleges are beginning to offer courses designed specifically for childcare workers. Residential childcare work is truly growing in prestige and popularity in the workforce at large. Childcare work is varied indeed; the childcare worker can never anticipate what will happen on shift and must be prepared for everything–good times and bad. Often this aspect is interesting to those who choose to make residential childcare work their profession. After working in residential childcare, it may be hard to imagine sitting behind a desk for a living. The childcare worker would be looking for much more variety and challenges requiring thinking on one's feet.

The job of a childcare worker involves providing care and supervision to minor clients at all times. Whether your clients are latency age or teens, the requirement to provide care and supervision remains the same. The childcare worker is responsible for supervising the children in the milieu (the therapeutic environment of the home itself), making sure they remain safe and their needs are met. On a typical day the childcare worker may pick the children up at school and return them to the facility, make sure they get their afternoon snack, assist with preparation of dinner, and supervise a study period while assisting children with their homework. Later in the evening, staff may watch television with residents, help them get prepare for school the next day, oversee bedtime hygiene routines, and enforce bedtime rules. During the course of the shift the childcare worker may be called upon to set limits or mediate disputes among residents. They may encounter an emergency situation, such as someone being absent without leave (AWOL) from the facility, and need to follow the facility's emergency protocols. On the other hand, staff may spend a good part of the evening interacting with the children, listening to the details of their day, offering advice and counsel, or just laughing, telling jokes, or having fun with the children as they all play a board game.

Although the childcare workers assume a "parental role" on shift, they are not the child's parents in any legal sense. They cannot make decisions for the children in care as they would their own children. State laws and regulations govern the decisions they are able to make. For example, as parents they might tell their own child to wait until morning to see if her minor stomach pain subsides; if a child in residential care asks to go to the emergency room for the same stomach pain, however, staff must take her. A parent-like decision is not appropriate because the childcare worker is not that child's legal guardian. Nevertheless, the childcare worker is the authority figure in charge when on shift and assumes the important responsibility of caring for the children, whether that involves setting a limit for behavior or making sure children do their homework and get to bed on time. As we will see, the structure, support and care given by the childcare worker is perhaps the most important element of residential treatment. It is the childcare workers who may have the most impact on the success or failure of the treatment of the children in their care.

Young children or teens in residential care are placed there because they have serious emotional and psychological issues. Many children in residential treatment have been tried in a variety of other settings before the high level of residential care was deemed necessary. They may have been placed with a relative (kinship care) or in foster homes with traditional foster parents. Another option that may have been tried is a foster family agency placement. In this type of setting, the foster parents are recruited and trained by the agency to foster children who have emotional problems. Different variations of lower level of care placements may have been tried several times, but each time the placement failed due to the emotional, behavioral, and psychological difficulties these children face. A relative or foster parent simply could not handle these children. Many times even foster parents who are specifically trained to deal with serious behavior issues are unable to meet the needs of these children. Youngsters are referred to residential treatment after other less-restrictive (in terms of structure and supervision) placements have been tried and failed.

A child in residential care may have a psychiatric diagnosis such as depression, posttraumatic stress disorder (PTSD), oppositional defiant disorder, conduct disorder, bipolar disorder, or a combination of diagnoses. He or she may also have a learning disorder or a combination of learning problems that make school especially challenging and may require placement in special classes and ongoing monitoring of progress. Residential care children may have development delays that cause their behavior to be inappropriate in a variety of settings and require remediation of the delays. Often, youngsters referred for residential care have exhibited behaviors that have been a concern in previous placements and the family home setting. They may have been violent toward self, family members, foster parents, staff at other facilities, peers, or property and may have a history of running away from home and/or placement. In many cases, children in placement have been victims of molestation, abuse, neglect, and/or abandonment. Because of their many issues children in care need the supervision, care, and guidance of childcare workers and others employed by a given facility. As these children become teenagers, they may not be able to make good decisions for themselves and especially require the protection and guidance of a team of trained professionals. The childcare worker is an important member of the team of supervisors, mental health professionals, and social workers who provide and oversee the treatment of each child.

The stories of clients' lives are often very tragic and sad. They have seen more hardship in their lives than we can imagine. Their parents may have been involved with drugs or alcohol and unable to care for and protect them. Sometimes a parent's own mental illness prevented her from parenting her child. Many of the children in placement have been there for many years and have moved around from one foster home to another and later from one group home to another. Sometimes youngsters, especially teens, arrive at a new placement having been at twenty or more placements in their short lives. It is no surprise that many kids in placement often feel no sense of attachment or belonging anywhere. Most of the children in residential care have been the victims of abuse, abandonment, neglect and/or molestation. Many have witnessed serious domestic violence. Childcare workers are charged with dealing with the resulting damage that occurred before the children came to their facility, and hopefully they can begin to help a child make some progress toward healing.

As you start your work as a childcare worker or if you are beginning to work at a new facility and certainly if you are a seasoned veteran, you probably have some understanding of the importance and challenges of working with children who require out of home placement. Dealing with acting out behaviors, depression, or other mood issues; eating disorders; and rivalries among peers day in and day out can be very difficult and stressful. Residential facilities have detailed polices and procedures to deal with whatever situation you may encounter. Most facilities offer training in crisis intervention to educate staff in techniques for managing escalating or out of control behavior. Fortunately, the good times keep us going–when a child is superexcited that he got a B on a test you helped him study for or a pair of feuding teen peers become friends again after a mediation with you. Often the simplest things provide the most smiles: watching a movie with the children, taking them to an amusement park, or playing a game of Monopoly. Many childcare workers are eager to work on Christmas morning to share in the joy and excitement of the children as they open their gifts. If you remain in the field for a number of years, you may begin to hear from former clients who are doing well and may even credit you with helping them get to that good place. For many childcare workers, nothing warms the heart more than hearing from a former client who is happy and contented with his or her life.

Of course, a large part of a residential facility is providing a home to the children, so you will also have to handle physical plant issues, such as running out of milk, the dishwasher not working, or a child accidentally or deliberately breaking a window. To assist you with your work, your facility's established program with guidelines, procedures, and protocols is there for you to use and follow. All childcare workers receive or will receive extensive training in all aspects of the program and its daily function. The training your facility offers covers a variety

of subjects from which key opens which lock, to driving ⸝
cles, to following house rules and consequences, to how to ⸝⸝
an emergency. Also, most facilities have senior staff and/or sup⸝
on shift or on call to help whenever needed.

In addition to program policies and procedures and physical p⸝
concerns, there are concepts that are important for all childcare workers. Understanding concepts that define your work will greatly assist
you in doing your job most effectively and providing the best service
possible to your clients. Learning about these concepts and how they
apply to your work offers guidelines for your behavior on the job and
allows you to better understand how to do your job and why the program works for your clients. Unfortunately, these vital concepts can be
difficult for supervisors to explain to their trainees. Concepts are not
concrete and tangible. A supervisor can show you where the extra fruit
juice is stored and which key opens the cabinet, but she or he may
have a hard time explaining what it means to have good boundaries
on the job. The purpose of this book is to teach you what you need to
know to be successful as a residential childcare worker. We will cover
in detail those concepts that are so important to your work, but are too
often skipped over during initial and ongoing training.

The cornerstone of a childcare worker's job is to provide milieu
therapy, and the important concepts you need to learn are all part of
milieu therapy. The following chapters will explain the meaning and
importance of milieu therapy and define your role as a practitioner of
milieu therapy. We will look in detail at some of the most important
components of milieu therapy: role modeling, boundaries, structure,
schedule, setting limits and rewards, and consistency. In addition, a
chapter will be devoted to emphasizing the importance of knowing
your milieu. Here we will explore some of the hidden resources that
you can use to become a better childcare worker and provide better
service to the children in your care. Of course, your initial training at
your facility went over the milieu in detail. You were shown where
things are stored, which key opens what lock, and where and how
medications are kept–the list goes on and on. What are the most important things to know about your milieu, however? We will examine
the answer to that question.

Later, we will discuss keeping yourself well in the midst of what
can be a very stressful and emotionally draining occupation. It is vital

that childcare workers keep themselves emotionally and physically healthy in order to avoid burnout. Taking your work home with you and failing to stay fit and eat well can take its toll when working in a stress-filled environment. Overall, understanding the concepts of milieu therapy and using the suggestions and techniques contained in this book will help to manage the stressors of the job.

Each chapter will conclude with a review of key points that were covered in the chapter. You can use the key points list as a quick reference when questions arise about your work. In addition, you can refer back to the review sections from time to time to refresh your recollection and understanding of the concepts covered in this book. At the end of each chapter there will also be one or more exercises that will assist you in one of several ways. Some exercises are designed to help you to better understand yourself, your role as a childcare worker, and your acceptance of that role. Others will help you to better understand the material covered in the chapter by providing review questions or scenarios to which you can apply what you have learned. Finally, some exercises will help you to apply the concepts you have learned to the facility where you work and the programs and structure

As we ask the children with whom we work to grow and change, so we as childcare workers must do the same. Learning more about the children with whom we work, the profession of childcare work, and residential care and improving how we do our job is essential as we continue to care for children so in need. Also important is a continuing effort to understand and improve oneself in order to move forward and become better at assisting the children in your care. Read on as the book is designed to help in all of these areas and more.

CHAPTER 1 REVIEW

1. Residential childcare work is a challenging and rewarding career that is growing in prestige and popularity.

2. Working as a residential childcare worker primarily involves providing care and supervision for children and also includes a variety of other tasks and responsibilities on each shift.

3. The childcare worker assumes a "parental role" in the children's lives but does not have the same legal right or decision-making abilities as a parent.

4. Children in residential care have serious emotional and psychological issues that require the structure and supervision of a residential facility.

5. The children in residential facilities are often the victims of abuse, abandonment, neglect, and/or molestation.

6. Dealing with acting-out behaviors that result from emotional, psychological and behavioral problems presents unique challenges for childcare workers.

7. Providing a well-functioning home for the children is another important responsibility for childcare workers.

8. The cornerstone of a childcare worker's job is providing milieu therapy, which includes the following important components: role modeling, boundaries, structure, the house schedule, setting limits, rewarding positive behavior, and consistency.

9. It is crucial that childcare workers employ wellness strategies to remain healthy while working in what can be a high-stress profession.

EXERCISE

Make a list of the qualities you possess that make you a good professional childcare worker. Try to list at least ten different qualities or characteristics. We will revisit your list in a later chapter.

1. _____

2. _____

3. _____

4. _____

5. _____

6. _____

7. _____

8. _____

9. _____

10. _____

Chapter 2

MILIEU THERAPY

Milieu therapy refers to the therapeutic environment of your program and the programmatic elements that are in place to assist clients with maintaining stability, healing from past trauma, and moving toward a more healthy emotional and psychological state. The program at your facility has been well-thought-out and planned by professionals in the field. Treatment is the focus of milieu therapy, and the programmatic elements and environment are designed to meet treatment goals. Something as small as a teenager's completing a daily chore is a part of a larger goal to teach that child how to take responsibility and eventually become able to care for herself. Other goals may involve larger issues such as learning to get along with others or managing mood swings. Each day in the milieu these goals are worked on and reached through hundreds of small interactions with the guidance and assistance of childcare workers.

In addition to the programmatic structure and procedures that you employ as a childcare worker, every interaction you have with a client becomes a component of milieu therapy with you as a practitioner of milieu therapy. James K. Whittaker precisely states the message of the milieu in his book *Caring for Troubled Children: Residential Treatment in a Community Context*:

> We accept you as a person with rights, feelings, and individuality; we reject, totally, those things you do which make trouble for yourself and for others and which keep you from growing as a competent, autonomous individual. We seek to create an environment where all the participants–children and staff–are interdependent, care about

one another, and are willing to challenge, support and aid each other in the process of growth and change. (1979, p. 85)

Helping a child learn to manage his anger when a situation arises at the facility may seem insignificant to some, but to that child it is a building block in a process that will help him become a better functioning adult. This is what milieu therapy does and what you provide as a milieu therapist and childcare worker.

At a small group home, childcare workers Margo and Julia reported for work to discover that two of the teenaged girls at the facility had a blowup earlier in the day. The girls, who had been best of friends, now hated each other and each threatened to beat up the other. The entire situation arose over a disagreement about whose turn it was to use a house computer game the girls particularly loved to play. The staff that Margo and Julia relieved had followed house policy to separate the girls and reinforced that the two were not to come close to each other for the remainder of the evening. Margo sat down with one of the girls and allowed her to tell her side of the story. Listening carefully, Margo let the girl get out all of her anger and frustration over the situation. Margo then suggested alternative ways of looking at the situation and different views of what might have motivated the girl's peer. Julia did the same with the other girl involved in the dispute.

For the next two days other childcare workers interacted with both girls in a similar fashion, reinforcing the messages that Margo and Julia had given them. After awhile, the girls realized they were getting similar messages from several staff they knew and trusted. They slowly began to take a different view of the situation that threatened to end their friendship. By the time the house social worker sat the girls down to do mediation to resolve the dispute, the girls announced that they had both apologized to the other and were now friends again. They also readily agreed that they would listen to the other girl's side before threatening violence and potentially losing the friendship. This is an example of milieu therapy at work. Childcare workers, through many small, individual interactions, send messages by word and example to teach youngsters, resolve disputes, and help children learn better coping skills among many other things. The children in this single example are well on their way to establishing better anger management and peer relationships, improved empathy, and enhanced problem-solving skills.

Milieu therapy is the cornerstone of the treatment of clients in your care. Think about it. Your clients see their therapist once a week or less, and they may only see their psychiatrist one time each month. They might see the program social worker a total of a few hours a week. However, they see childcare workers every single day they are in placement. More importantly, they interact with each childcare worker for the extended period of time that makes up that childcare worker's shift. That close daily contact with you and your colleagues provides the opportunity for some of the most significant progress toward healthy living and independence. As James Harris writes in his book *Respecting Residential Work With Children,* "Direct care staff members have the most interaction with children in residential placement. This means they have the greatest potential impact on building relationships with youth in their care" (2003, p. 22). The work of a childcare worker is important stuff. Never feel that you are at the bottom of the food chain in the your organization. Any executive director or manager will know how important your efforts are, and so should you.

ELEMENTS OF MILIEU THERAPY

Much of milieu therapy involves setting up and maintaining structure for your clients. The program runs as it runs, it remains consistent and fair, and you help to keep it going. The structure of the program provides your clients with a sense of safety. Whereas their early lives may have been filled with chaos, your program structure shows them a different way, a calmer more consistent way of living. Within the sense of safety and consistency, clients may begin to work on their issues, their schoolwork, their relationships, and their behavior.

The house schedule is an important element of maintaining the overall structure, which is so important to milieu therapy. Your adherence to the house schedule reinforces structure and overall safety for your clients. After early lives filled with uncertainty, clients respond favorably to knowing what will happen throughout the day and when. They feel secure and comforted. In addition, the schedule is designed to provide, depending on your level of care, a variety of activities; scheduled responsibilities, such as phone time or shower times; as well as specific periods of free time. Your manager or other staff at your facility designs the schedule to provide balanced structure and use of time, including positive leisure activities.

If you are going to work successfully as a childcare worker you must have and maintain good boundaries. Your personal life must be kept separate and left at the door when you enter your workplace. You must maintain a professional demeanor and work only within your scope of practice. The quickest way to undermine the effectiveness of your program's milieu therapy is if one or more staff are operating with poor boundaries. When you come to work as a milieu therapist, it must be all about the children. Childcare workers with poor boundaries take the focus away from the children and put it on themselves. Although in most cases this shift of focus is unintentional, it is nonetheless countertherapeutic, taking away from the work you need to do for the children in your care.

Another important part of milieu therapy is limit setting. Your job as a childcare worker often involves setting limits and assigning consequences for negative behaviors. It is vital that your clients learn that there are consequences for negative behavior. Setting limits for behaviors helps to maintain a safe and secure environment for all clients where negative behavior is not condoned.

Childcare workers must also reward positive behavior. Rewarding good behavior is equally as important as setting limits for negative behaviors is. A good program will have elements of consequences as well as rewards. Many of the children in residential care were not rewarded for being good, and so they seek attention through behaving poorly. As a childcare worker you have the opportunity to teach them that it feels good to be good. You are also helping one baby step at a time to raise their self-esteem, which can often be quite low for these children. Above all, it is vital that childcare workers ensure that rewards and consequences are given out fairly and equally.

Many children in placement come from homes where there was domestic violence, dysfunctional relationships and communication, verbally abusive family members, and untrustworthy parental figures. As a result, they may not have learned effective communication skills. They may not trust adults or authority figures. Often, our clients do not understand how to have and maintain healthy relationships with peers or adults, especially when they spent their early years living amid the dysfunction of their parents' lives. An important component of milieu therapy involves teaching your clients effective communication and relationship building through role modeling appropriate behavior.

As a childcare worker, you are also role modeling healthy adult behavior for your clients. Some of them may never have had the opportunity to experience healthy behavior by an authority figure. In essence, your role modeling of healthy adult behavior teaches them how an adult behaves, giving them a reference that they can use when approaching adulthood. Your clients will be watching you. They will take note of how you carry yourself, how you communicate, and how you handle your authority. As they watch, they learn. You are teaching them in little ways and big ways how to behave.

Creating an environment in which consistency rules is another cornerstone of milieu therapy. Your clients will feel safe and secure knowing that their house is consistent and fair. In return, they will begin to respect the program and the staff. Inconsistency breeds mistrust and undermines your clients' sense of safety. It is important that your clients know that the rules, policies, and procedures are applied fairly, consistently, and evenly. As a childcare worker you should never play favorites or allow your emotions to cloud your consistent application of your program's structure.

In the next six chapters, we will examine the major components of milieu therapy more closely. These are the concepts you need to know to do your job most effectively. Crucial to your success as a childcare worker is an understanding of these concepts and putting that understanding to good use as you work with your clients. As an added benefit, learning about these elements of milieu therapy will help you to avoid and/or manage stressful situations more effectively. This makes things better for your clients and for you.

CHAPTER 2 REVIEW

1. Milieu therapy refers to the therapeutic environment of a residential program. Milieu therapy assists children with maintaining stability, healing from past trauma, and moving toward a more healthy emotional and psychological state.

2. Every interaction a childcare worker has with a client becomes a component of milieu therapy with the childcare worker as a practitioner of milieu therapy.

3. The daily contact childcare workers have with children in care provides opportunity for some of the most significant progress toward treatment goals for each individual child in care.

4. The job of the childcare worker is a very important one. The milieu therapy provided by childcare workers has the most direct and significant effect on children in residential care.

5. Much of milieu therapy involves setting up and maintaining structure for children. The structure of a program offers children a sense of safety and consistency.

6. An important element of maintaining overall structure, the house schedule reinforces structure and overall safety for children.

7. Maintaining good boundaries is essential for success as a childcare worker. Poor boundaries create confusion and uncertainty for children and can lead to burnout for childcare workers.

8. A therapeutic milieu is one in which childcare workers set limits for negative behaviors and assign consequences for rule violations.

9. Childcare workers must also reward positive behavior to teach children that it feels good to be good.

10. Childcare workers teach children through role modeling. Children learn things such as good communication skills, healthy adult behavior, and relationship building.

11. Consistency is critical to a successful therapeutic milieu. Inconsistency breeds mistrust and undermines the sense of safety.

12. An understanding of the major components of milieu therapy is crucial to success for a childcare worker. How well a staff of childcare workers grasps these concepts may determine the success or failure of the program as a whole.

EXERCISES

Before we start looking in greater detail at the elements of milieu therapy that are so important to the success of a childcare worker and, indeed, the residential program as a whole, let us take a look at how well you feel you are doing in each of them. Be as honest as you can. You might want to consider feedback you have received from coworkers and supervisors when making your ranking. We will look at your numbers again after the chapter on each element of milieu therapy.

Next to each element below rank yourself using a scale from 1 to 3 as follows:

1–Need additional training and work to be successful
2–Fine, but could use improvement
3–Element mastered, but still would like to learn to be even better

1. Program Structure: _____

2. The House Schedule: _____

3. Maintaining Good Boundaries: _____

4. Limit Setting: _____

5. Rewarding Positive: _____

6. Role Modeling: _____

7. Consistency: _____

Now list three things that you would like to improve in your own personal work as a childcare worker. Once again, you might want to consider feedback you have gotten from coworkers and supervisors. Feedback from the children in your care may also be relevant.

1. _____

2. _____

3. _____

Chapter 3

ELEMENTS OF MILIEU THERAPY: PROGRAM STRUCTURE

I magine you are eight years old and living with a mother addicted to crystal methamphetamine. Your father is unknown or not involved in your life. You have only your mother to depend on.

Mother lives in a motel room and pays week to week. The room is dirty and more times than not there is little or no food. She is unable to work because of her drug habit and the burden of dealing with you and your two siblings: one two years younger than you are and one an infant. Mother screams and cries all the time because she has no money.

Your baby brother wails constantly, most likely because mother used methamphetamines throughout her pregnancy. Mother yells at him to stop crying. Sometimes she shakes him so hard that you have to beg her not to hurt your baby brother. She responds by shoving you across the room, calling you a little bitch, and threatening to beat your ass until it is raw.

People come and go at all hours of the night. Often three or four different people sleep there. Sometimes they stay up all night and you cannott sleep at all. A couple of times some of the visitors got into fist-fights, and you grabbed your brother and sister, ran into the bath-room, shut the door, and hid until it was quiet again. One of the men whom Mother told you to call uncle makes you sit on his lap, and you feel very afraid and uncomfortable. Mother often leaves and is gone for days, and you have to do your best to take care of your siblings. You love school, but you hardly ever go because Mother never feels like taking you. Besides, she needs you to take care of your brother and sister.

All Mother thinks about is her drugs. When she runs out and cannot get any, she goes crazy. You are afraid she might kill you or your siblings. One time she grabbed a belt and kept hitting your sister until her back was bloody. Sometimes when she has run out of methamphetamines, strange men come over, and Mother sends you to a neighbor's room. Once when you came back Mother had a black eye and bloody nose.

Many nights you are so scared and sad that you cry yourself to sleep. Mother screams at you when you do this, so you have learned to muffle your sobs with your pillow.

This scenario describes the chaos and danger within which many of our children lived before they were removed from their homes or they got into trouble with the law and were put on probation. As you might imagine, children exposed to these or similar conditions experience fear, anger, and confusion. The sad fact is that children raised in these types of environments suffer emotional, sexual, and physical abuse; abandonment; and neglect. The effects are serious and far reaching, including "enduring distortions in relationship patterns, subjective experience, sense of self, and coping strategies" (Bleiberg, 2001, p. 85). Many psychological conditions may result, such as PSTD, oppositional defiant disorder, drug or alcohol dependency, depression, anxiety disorders, and characterological disorders, such as borderline personality disorder or conduct disorder. When children are removed from their family home, they unfortunately are very damaged children with many behavioral and psychological issues. These children need caring adults to provide for their needs and allow them to work on their many treatment issues in a safe environment.

In order for our clients to feel safe and have the ability to work on healing, milieu therapy provides a therapeutic structure within which they live. Therapeutic structure consists of your program's rules, policies, procedures, and program schedule. The structure of your facility forms a kind of wall of safety around each child. Most bad things cannot get in, and each child's behaviors are contained and handled therapeutically inside. Within the walls is a place where they can feel secure, work on their issues, and begin to feel okay. When childcare workers do their part to keep cracks from occurring in the wall (therapeutic structure), there is hope for healing.

Therapeutic structure is in sharp contrast to the chaos of many of our clients' home lives. Within the therapeutic structure, clients know what will happen at any given time, they understand that there are rules to follow and limits on their behavior, and they know that limits will be set and rewards will be given in a fair and appropriate manner. Food will be served as scheduled, and they will never go hungry. A warm bed is provided for them to sleep in, and their personal belongings surround them in their own personal space. No one will scream and yell at them; on the contrary, caring people are there to listen when they want someone to talk to. Their medical concerns will be handled in a timely manner. They go to school each day, and staff will keep abreast of their progress and offer help when needed. The program structure of the milieu "consists of a way of structuring daily life defined by explicit rules and expectations that give predictability and consistency to interactions with peers and staff" (Bleiberg, 2001, p. 237).

In the therapeutic milieu, clients are encouraged to explore their own interests in school and otherwise. The calm, chaos-free environment allows them to leave survival mode and move toward self-improvement and self-enhancement. They learn to become more comfortable with themselves. At your program, they can be kids, perhaps for the first time in their lives. Your therapeutic milieu offers fun activities and recreation. Toys, games, and computers are available for them to use. Age-appropriate books and magazines are everywhere. For the first time in their lives, they can explore, function, and begin to learn to feel good about themselves, knowing that all of their needs are taken care of. As James Whittaker points out, "A therapeutic milieu is a specifically designed environment in which the events of daily living are used as formats for teaching competence in basic life skills. The living environment becomes both a means and a context for growth and change" (Whitaker, 1979, p. 36). Through the structure of the milieu, children can begin to heal and develop in their lives.

It is imperative that you as a childcare worker understand the great importance of strongly maintaining the safe, fertile ground of the therapeutic milieu. You must keep that wall of safety intact for your clients in order for them to have the opportunity for growth and change. Cracks may appear in the wall if the structure of your program is not maintained, and the consequences for the children in your care can be quite serious. Here are some suggestions on how to do your part in keeping the program structure intact:

1. Always maintain a professional demeanor while on shift
2. Use and follow program rules, consequences, and reward systems
3. Adhere to program policies and procedures
4. Listen to direction and counsel of supervisors
5. Recognize that the schedule is the backbone of the program and never deviate without permission from a supervisor

PROFESSIONAL DEMEANOR

Your enforcement of program structure begins with having a positive, calm demeanor whenever you are at work. Leave your emotional baggage at the door and assume a professional mindset the minute you walk inside. In many ways, you are like a nurse caring for a seriously ill patient in a hospital. A good nurse never complains about her back hurting or having a bad day to her patients. She does not complain to the patient about the hospital, the doctors, or the other nurses. She does not gossip about other patients. When she is at work, she is concerned with her patient first and making him or her feel as comfortable as possible.

Similarly, at a residential facility, it is all about your clients. It is not about you and your needs; it is about your clients and their needs. Your clients need you to be positive and caring. They need you to listen to them and meet their needs to the best of your ability within the program's policies. You cannot do that if you are focused on your own concerns or, worse, if you put those concerns on the children. If you appear upset or distracted to the children, a crack begins to appear in the wall of safety. The children may begin to act out because memories may be triggered of their life before placement, when it was never about them and always about their inadequate caregiver.

As you know, or will find out, despite the contrast with their home life, your clients for the most part will resent being in placement. How would you feel if you were removed from your home–no matter how justified authorities were in doing so? Our children are confused, hurt, angry, and resentful, and they long for the home from which they were removed no matter how unhealthy an environment it was. Many times their anger will be directed at you and your coworkers. A calm, caring, positive demeanor will go a long way in diffusing these feelings when they flare up. If you come to work grumpy and out of sorts, you will only fan the flames of your clients' negative feelings.

To maintain a positive demeanor while on shift, always remember the caring nurse tending to her patients. Think of how you would want her to treat you and treat the children in your care the same. All of us have problems from time to time. Some days we just do not feel as well as others. Of course, nurses do, too, but they still have to be there for their patients. If you find that you are having difficulty staying calm and positive on a particular shift, take a break and allow your coworkers to interact with the children. Return to the milieu when you feel refreshed and ready to get back to the business of caring for your clients.

PROGRAM RULES, CONSEQUENCES, AND REWARD SYSTEM

Central to your program's structure is the system of rules, consequences and rewards. You will want to become very familiar with your program's house rules as soon as possible. Once you have a good working knowledge of the house rules, you should move on to learn the consequences and rewards system. If you are new at childcare work or new to the facility, you should refrain from handing out rewards or consequences without consulting with a senior staff until your knowledge is solid. Even after you are comfortable with the rewards and consequences, it is a good idea to check the lists before handing out rewards or consequences. Many experienced staff sometimes must consult the listing of rules consequences and rewards to clarify for themselves in the moment.

Your facility's rules and consequences are meant to keep order and to teach—not to punish. If you find a child's breaking of a rule is making you angry or upset, you are taking things too personally and your calm demeanor will be broken. Remember consequences are given to show children that there are natural consequences for negative behavior. This lesson will be important for the rest of their lives. Once again, these small steps of learning chip away at years of inappropriate guidance from their adult caregivers. You, as milieu therapist, are teaching and contributing to their growth as individuals.

When Jack arrived on shift at the boys' facility where he worked, he walked into the staff office and found his coworker Brian sitting at a desk dashing off some notes in one of the boy's charts. Brian looked up and said, "Thank goodness. Maybe you can talk some sense into that little monster out there."

A seasoned childcare worker, Jack immediately knew that something was amiss with his usually solid coworker. "What's going on?" he asked.

Brian began to explain about a particular boy's disrespectful and mischievous behavior over the past hour. "Then he picked up an apple and threw it against the wall, so I'm giving him consequences," Brian said. "I'm sorry to say I might have raised my voice when I was talking to him before coming into the office."

Jack could see that Brian's blood was just about at the boiling point. His face was red and his tone of voice conveyed anger. Reminding him of the importance of remaining calm and maintaining a professional demeanor, Jack offered to handle the process of assigning consequences and speaking to the boy. Brian realized immediately that Jack was right and soon recognized that some family problems he was having were interfering with his ability to stay professional in his interactions with the children. He made a mental note to make an appointment with his personal counselor to discuss coping strategies and to discuss his current issues with his supervisor. He quickly explained and apologized to Jack, but Jack told him not to worry. "It happens to the best of us some time or another," he told Brian.

When Jack left the office to talk to the boy with whom Brian had the conflict, he was not surprised to find the rest of the boys acting out. The children were running around the house throwing water at each other from paper cups. Colin, the childcare worker on the floor, was desperately trying to calm the children. He looked at Jack for assistance. Jack knew that the children had begun to feel unsafe because of Brian's break in his professional demeanor and realized that normalcy must be reestablished as quickly as possible. He calmly asked each of the boys individually to meet him at the back door of the house and be ready for a game of kickball. The boys loved the idea. "There's nothing like a little exercise to calm these boys down," he told Colin, who watched carefully as Jack handled the situation using his calm, professional demeanor. Absorbed in their game the boys' behavior changed, and they were calm and compliant for the remainder of the day.

It is of the utmost importance that you apply the rules consistently, fairly and evenly in the course of each of your shifts. Children rely on that consistency and will be on the lookout for inconsistencies— both in your application of rules and consequences and the way you assign consequences from one child to another. If you lose your cool, you are more likely to act in a punitive manner and hand out consequences to punish rather than to instruct. Maintaining the calm, professional demeanor will greatly assist you in keeping your cool and approaching rules and consequences in a fair and consistent manner.

ADHERENCE TO YOUR PROGRAM'S POLICIES AND PROCEDURES

When you received your initial training at your facility, you were introduced to an array of policies and procedures, such as emergency protocols, borrowing and lending between clients, and client use of sharp objects. Someone who has many years of experience working in residential treatment designs each policy or procedure at your facility for a specific purpose. The backdrop of policies and procedures forms another important component in the structure of your facility's program. You must learn and practice all policies and procedures and follow them at all times whenever you are on shift. Disregarding policies and procedures can lead to a disintegration of the program's structure and, in certain cases, can even place clients in danger.

It is useful to remind yourself before every shift that your job is serious business. Your clients have emotional and psychological issues that require your vigilance. Always remain professional, always be watchful, and never let your guard down. Keep your program policies and procedures uppermost in your mind.

Many times a shift can almost feel like you are not really at work. You are watching television with the children, playing games, laughing, and chatting. Becoming lulled by the recreational aspect of your job, you may begin to reconsider the program's polices and procedures. "Why shouldn't I give Mary her razor even though she's on safety watch? She seems fine to me," you might ask yourself. You may think, "Jane's been good all day. Why can't I let her watch television even though she's on restriction?" These are just two of many scenarios that could lead to your questioning and not following your program's policies and procedures.

In the case of Mary's safety watch, giving her a razor while she is on safety watch is dangerous. She could use it to harm herself or others. She is on safety watch for a reason; she is not permitted to have sharp objects for a reason. A team of professionals has decided to place her on safety watch because of her real potential to harm herself or others. The team is aware of Mary's history as well as recent events and at least one member of the team, and maybe an outside psychiatrist or other mental health professional, has assessed Mary and determined that she should be placed on safety watch. Your observation of her based on your experience with her during a single shift is not sufficient to make the determination that safety watch is no longer needed. The procedure of safety watch is in place to protect the client and others. What you observed on your shift with Mary simply indicates that the policy is working and does not need to be changed until the treatment team can reassess her.

The second example operates with a great deal more subtlety. If you disregard program policy and let Jane watch television while on restricted privileges, clients will see the unfairness and feel as if you are favoring Jane. Others will note the break in structure and will expect the same treatment from you and perhaps even other staff members. You are left with some clients harboring negative feelings and others who will use your error in judgment to manipulate you and other staff members in the future. A breakdown in program structure has occurred, and clients begin to feel unsafe. You may start to see acting out behaviors on this or future shifts.

Although it may appear as if Jane initially appreciates your gesture, she knows what you have done is against program policy. Ultimately, she will have less respect for you, and your other clients will perceive your actions as favoritism. Peers may feel an emotional wound reopened because of your action, for it is highly likely that they experienced rejection as a result of favoritism in their pasts. Your clients have a firm grasp of program rules, and they will watch with hypervigilance for any hint of unfairness or favoritism when you apply those rules.

If you do not understand a particular policy or procedure, ask your supervisor for clarification and/or explanation. It is okay to go to a supervisor and say, "I don't understand why we are required to follow safe watch protocols when the client seems fine on my shift. Could you give me more information, so I can better understand?" Most supervisors will be more than happy to explain in detail why any particular policy or procedure is in place. Your supervisor would rather help you understand than to have to deal with the fallout from a break in program structure.

DIRECTION AND COUNSEL OF SUPERVISORS

Your supervisors have a thorough knowledge of your program's structural components and a solid experience with clients and their families. Especially if you are new to the field of residential treatment, it is very important that you seek and follow the direction and advice of your supervisors. If you have experience in the field but are new to your current facility, your supervisor will have knowledge of your particular facility that you do not. Seeking his or her advice and following directions will help get you on board much faster with your new program.

Do not be afraid to "hang back" at first and allow senior staff to take the lead on your shift until you get a better feel for the program and clients. A good supervisor will actually advise you to do this. There is a lot to learn, myriad little details to absorb. No one expects that you will have it all down when you work your first couple of weeks of shifts. Although your job knowledge is solidifying, let senior staff take the lead to ensure that you do not make errors that could upset the program structure.

THE HOUSE SCHEDULE

The most important aspect of day-to-day program structure is the daily schedule. Your clients' lives revolve around that schedule. It gives them a sense of safety and security within which they can live and work on their issues and responsibilities. Even a minor unauthorized deviation in the schedule can upset your clients and result in their feeling unsafe. A serious crack will occur in the wall of safety around them.

Because the schedule is so critical to a program's success, the next chapter will discuss the schedule in detail so that you can understand its importance, how to effectively adhere to the schedule, and the pitfalls of failing to follow the schedule.

CHAPTER 3 REVIEW

1. Children in residential facilities most often have histories that involve chaotic and extremely dysfunctional living situations.

2. The therapeutic structure creates a wall of safety around each child within which they can live, work on their issues, and just be kids.

3. The therapeutic structure consists of your program's policies and procedures and the house schedule.

4. Within the therapeutic structure children know what will happen at any given time and that their needs will always be met.

5. It is imperative that childcare workers understand the importance of strongly maintaining the safe, fertile ground of the therapeutic milieu.

6. In order to preserve the structure of the milieu, childcare workers must always maintain a professional demeanor while on shift. Personal issues and problems must be left outside the door prior to entering for your shift.

7. Another structure preserver is adherence to your program's rules, consequences, and reward system. Learn them well and apply them consistently and fairly at all times.

8. Your facility's policies and procedures must be learned and studied thoroughly. Throughout every shift that you work, you must remain mindful of the policies and procedures and follow them at all times in all situations. This is the most important aspect of maintaining structure.

9. If you do not understand anything about your facility's structure, seek the advice and counsel of your supervisors. They
   will be more than willing to help you because they know how
   crucial a solid program structure is to the well-being of the children in your care.

10. Finally, the house schedule is the backbone of structure each
    day. Adherence to the schedule is critical to the day-to-day
    maintenance of program structure.

EXERCISE

Make a list of the five most important elements of structure at your
facility. Then explain how each one works to provide children with a
sense of safety and security.

1. Element:

   Importance:

2. Element:

   Importance:

3. Element:

   Importance:

4. Element:

   Importance:

5. Element:

   Importance:

Chapter 4

ELEMENTS OF MILIEU THERAPY:
THE HOUSE SCHEDULE

The house schedule forms the backbone of the daily structure at your facility. It is the framework upon which the day rests. It represents the basis for consistency and comforting predictability for the children in your care. Drafting the house schedule is no small affair. A team of people at your facility carefully prepares your facility's schedule. Managers, social workers, therapists, and executive directors give input. Suggestions by case managers, county social workers, probation officers, or mental health caseworkers are given close consideration. Requirements specified by your facility's licensing regulations are included.

Compiling the schedule is a complex job that takes into account many factors. Medical appointments, meetings with social workers and other advocates, school activities, special classes, visits, and passes are just a few of the items that may be regularly included. Care is also taken to include time for varied and enjoyable recreational activities. Meal and snack times are listed on the schedule as well as free time periods. In his book *A Guide for Child-Care Workers*, Dr. Morris Fritz Mayer describes the relevance of scheduling in the therapeutic milieu:

All institutions are based on the assumption that education, treatment and growing up are a twenty-four hour-a-day business, so that everything in daily life becomes a means toward the goal of bringing about a healthy, well-integrated, social functioning individual. Many things that have to be done, like cleaning, laundering and keeping the cottage in order are not important only for the smooth functioning of the institution, but also for the smooth functioning of the child himself now and in the future. (1958, pp. 78–79)

At your facility, the house schedule has been carefully designed to meet your clients' needs. For children coming to residential placement from lives where chaos and uncertainty reigned, perhaps the aspect having the most impact on milieu therapy is the structure and security your program's daily schedule provides. The facility schedule offers "structure, predictability, and a sense of safety in the sometimes scary world of a troubled child. In fact, the more troubled a child is, the more critical is the need for routines, and the more tightly administered they should be" (Appelstein, 1998, p. 73).

Staff should never underestimate the power of the house schedule in the overall scheme of the treatment that is provided at your facility.

THE BENEFITS OF A HOUSE SCHEDULE

Most children entering a new residential placement for the first time do so with a great deal of fear and trepidation. They do not know any of the adults or peers at the facility; they do not know how things work or operate the facility. New children at a given facility may have anxiety over whether or not their basic needs will be met. Many of the children with whom you work enter your program with a lot of anxiety. Likely, they are asking themselves some of these questions:

1. Can I trust these people to follow through and do what they say they're going to do?
2. Will food be available when I'm hungry?
3. Will food be available when I'm hungry tomorrow?
4. Can I see the doctor when I'm sick?
5. Am I able to go to school every day?
6. Will I be able to get to school on time?
7. Is there going to be quiet time to do my homework or read a book or color a picture?
8. Will I get to bed at a decent hour and will someone wake me in the morning so I can get to school?
9. Do I have time to talk to people about what's bothering me?
10. Will I have the chance to do fun activities?

The house schedule answers all of these questions and more. Every day, breakfast, lunch, dinner, and snack time appear on the schedule. Bedtime and wake-up times are listed every day. Homework time is scheduled several days each week. Free time is blocked off for your clients every day or almost every day. Time is allotted for using the phone, watching television, playing games, or attending recreational and community activities. When they read it each morning and learn that it is followed day after day, the daily schedule actually becomes a source of comfort for troubled children.

The well-followed schedule tells clients: your needs will be met consistently and regularly and with care and consideration for your well-being. Within the structure that the schedule provides, your clients begin to feel safe and secure. In a life without chaos or constant change and instability, they can focus on their schoolwork, their treatment issues, and just being a kid. The milieu's schedule "provides a safe, predictable environment for people to work on their problems" (Crone, 1984, p. 56).

If your facility posts a daily schedule, you will quickly notice that your clients not only read it, but also can tell you what is on the schedule and ask questions about items that appear there. They will often refer back to the schedule several times a day. The schedule offers consistency and certainty. They can relax knowing what will happen at any given time each day.

At a group home for teenaged boys, residents woke up and most days looked at the newly posted daily schedule even before eating their breakfast. One boy named Michael was particularly interested in the schedule. The morning staff became used to being asked many questions by Michael as soon as he read the schedule. "What is that doctor's appointments for me about?" he would ask, even though the program manager had completely explained the appointment to him when it was made. He also asked questions about food: what is the two o'clock snack today or can you tell me whether I can have juice with my eight o'clock snack? His questions were numerous and regular but staff patiently answered them every day. One evening at the facility's staff meeting, a morning staff member happened to remark about Michael's schedule questions. "The other boys ask questions once and awhile, but Michael asks four or five every day," the childcare worker told the group. The program social worker told the staff that Michael had come from a very troubled background. His mother was mentally ill and often they lived on the streets. He frequently went hungry and was often left alone while his mother wandered the streets aimlessly. Michael had shared with the social worker that almost every day he feared that his mother would not find her way back to him. Sometimes, in fact, she did not, and he would be alone for days. "More than likely," the social worker told the staff, "Michael checks and rechecks the schedule to prove to himself that everything is going to stay regular and consistent and that his needs will continue to be met every day." Staff realized that what they thought were insignificant questions were really very important for Michael's sense of well-being. The childcare workers and the house schedule were doing exactly what Michael needed.

THE IMPORTANCE OF FOLLOWING THE HOUSE SCHEDULE

When you consider the importance the schedule has in the lives of your clients, you may begin to see that the schedule must be followed to the letter as best as possible. If an item on the schedule cannot be completed, for example, an outdoor event when there is rain, you should call and consult your supervisor about suggestions for alternate activities and permission to deviate from the schedule. You should never change the schedule yourself for any reason without the permission of your supervisor.

If you arbitrarily deviate from the schedule, you may be taking your clients' sense of structure and safety away. The children in your care will not know what will happen and when on any given day. They will quickly realize that they cannot trust what you and other staff say and do. Your clients may feel they will no longer be able to count on their needs being met. The threat of a return to the chaos of their earlier lives becomes a real possibility.

As their sense of safety begins to unravel over time, clients will return to behaviors that worked for them in chaotic living situations: manipulating, lying, stealing, hoarding food, acting out, or acting in a passive-aggressive manner. You may see an increase in or return of tantrums in a child who had been making progress in that area. School grades may suffer and progress in therapy may be at a stalemate.

Sound like an exaggeration? What follows is an example of what can happen if a single staff person does not follow the schedule.

Marjorie, a new childcare worker at Mortimer's group home for teen boys, went through an extensive training and on the job shadowing of senior staff. At the end of her training she passed a test that measured the knowledge she had acquired. Always a leader, she soon became the lead childcare worker on shift. She loved her job and felt a lot of compassion for her clients.

The one thing she never understood at her job was what she called the "too rigid schedule." She liked to be spontaneous, to do things on the spur of the moment. The house schedule simply did not fit her style.

One hot day in July after a scheduled trip to a local swimming pool, she decided it would be fun to treat her clients to ice cream. Although her coworker voiced a concern, Marjorie insisted it was not a problem. When they pulled up to the ice cream stand, Marjorie asked everyone to stop and listen to her. "I'm giving you a special treat today," she told them. "I know it's not on the schedule, but you deserve it. Just don't tell Harris (her supervisor) about this or I'll get in trouble and we won't be able to do this again."

As the children were exiting the van, Marjorie grabbed her coworker's arm and said, "That means you, too. If we want to be able to give the kids special treats, you can't tell our boss, okay?"

Even though she felt uneasy, the coworker agreed, not wanting to be a snitch. The two staff followed the children up to the ice cream stand. Everyone had a great time.

The next day Marjorie was not on shift, but the staff on duty had to handle the beginning of the damage Marjorie's actions had caused. After an outing to a movie, the children began to beg relentlessly to stop for ice cream on the way home.

"I'm sorry, but we can't do that," childcare worker Helen responded. " You all know it's not on the schedule."

One of the boys piped up and said, "We know, but other staff let us go get ice cream all the time. It's okay to do it."

Helen asked, "Who let's you do that all the time?"

The boy responded, "Everybody else does. You're the only mean one who says no."

Helen replied, "I'm sorry, but on my shift I follow the rules."

"That's because you're a bitch," the boy lashed back.

Helen kept her cool and continued driving. "I'm sorry you feel that way, but if you continue to use bad language, I'll have to give you a consequence."

The boy did not stop cussing and consequences were given. Once back at home, the boy was so angry over being denied a treat and getting consequences that his behavior deteriorated, and he received more consequences. His attitude toward the house and the staff began to sour. He began to feel that they did not care about him and treated him unfairly. Soon he was talking to the other boys about his changed attitude and discovered some of them felt the same way. An infectious negative attitude was taking over the house. Soon the children begin to dislike staff that followed the schedule while loving their friend and childcare worker Marjorie. (This situation will backfire on Marjorie, as you will see in a later chapter.)

As you can see, the break in the schedule becomes a bargaining chip for manipulation and splitting of staff. This is possible because the deviation from the schedule becomes a crack (and a rather large one) in the wall of safety around the children. Because the children begin to expect deviation from the schedule, they become upset and angry when they do not get what they want. They act out and consequences result. Soon they begin to feel unsafe. The children wonder if they can trust anyone at their facility and if anyone there will follow through with anything. They are confused by Marjorie, who on the one hand gives them treats but on the other hand asks them to lie for her. Life at the group home begins to mirror the dysfunction of the homes from which they were removed.

DIFFICULTIES WITH THE HOUSE SCHEDULE PRACTICE

Why do some childcare workers change the schedule they were trained to follow? Here are some of the many reasons given:

1. The schedule is too rigid. I just can't follow it.
2. I like to be spontaneous.
3. I want the kids to like me and giving them special treats will help make them like me.

4. I don't understand why more special treats are not included on the schedule

Once again, the previous examples are all about the childcare worker and not about the children he or she serves. As a childcare worker, you must put the needs and best interests of the children in your care first. Your own wants and needs are not relevant. Your work is about the children, not about you. Remember the analogy comparing a childcare worker to a nurse. A nurse does not come to work thinking about his or her own needs and trying to get those needs met through his or her patients. A nurse does not question the structure of her ward or floor or hospital. Instead, she follows the procedures knowing that they are in place to serve the best interests of her patients.

Difficulty #1: The House Schedule Is Too Rigid

Childcare workers who feel that the schedule is too rigid to follow not only are thinking about their own needs over those of the children, but also may have a problem with following instruction and authority. More than likely they are confusing their personal life with their work life. Nurses do not get to decide when they feel like giving their patients their medication, nor do childcare workers have the authority to decide how the house schedule should be constructed.

Difficulty #2: I Like To Be Spontaneous

Once again, workers who feel they cannot follow the schedule because they like to be spontaneous are confusing work life and personal life. Spontaneity is a wonderful quality and in their own lives probably serves them very well, but at work it will have negative consequences for the children in their care. The children require consistency and predictability not spontaneity.

Difficulty #3: I Want the Children To Like Me and Giving Them Special Treats Will Help Make Them Like Me

Any good supervisor will instinctively suspect a childcare worker who wants the children to like him or her needs some additional training to understand the true nature of his or her role with the children.

Many new childcare workers start out wanting the children to like them, but most quickly realize that an authority figure is not always liked but hopefully is always respected. Unfortunately, some childcare workers are so focused on getting their own needs met that they never make the transition to putting the children's needs first. These individuals may not be appropriate for work in this field or may need some sessions with a therapist to understand and remediate this issue before returning to work with children.

Difficulty #4: I Don't Understand Why More Special Treats Are Not Included on the Schedule

A childcare worker who does not understand why there are not more treats on the schedule may need additional training. This worker does not understand the process of making the schedule and the many things that need to be scheduled and taken into consideration. Treats, such as ice cream cones in the case of Marjorie's break from the schedule, may be infrequently included due to dietary concern. In fact, many children who have been molested tend to have issues with their weight. They may use food for comfort and the additional weight may psychologically form a barrier between them and the outside world. Other children on psychotropic medications may be dealing with a common side effect of many such medications—weight gain. In these cases, it is important to watch food intake, especially high-calorie food. It is also important that food not be used as a reward for good behavior because this may only encourage the use of food for comfort.

HELP WITH FOLLOWING THE HOUSE SCHEDULE

If you do not understand the importance of your house schedule and its formulation process, talk to your supervisor. Hopefully, your supervisor will be able to answer any questions you may have so that you can more confidently perform your job. Think of the house schedule as a guide and safety net for you as well as your clients. The schedule can be viewed as a separate entity that you must obey as you do your job. A lot of manipulation can be nipped in the bud by referring to the schedule: "It's not personal; it's the schedule and I have to follow it when I'm doing my job." When the children beg to stop at a the mall on the way home from a doctor's appointment or ask if you can take them to get a coffee drink on the way home from school, you need only say, "I'm sorry, but you know I can't because it's not on the schedule." The children will understand this right away because they have heard it from you and other staff, and the request will be dropped relatively quickly.

In this way, you are not the "bad guy." You are simply doing your job and following the rules and guidelines of your employment. Think about what a wonderful piece of role modeling that is for your clients. You are a confident adult who lives within the rules and abides by them with calm assuredness and a strong sense of fairness. That is what serving your clients is all about.

CHAPTER 4 REVIEW

1. The house schedule is carefully prepared by a team of people at your facility, taking into account a variety of needs, factors, and responsibilities.

2. The house schedule shows children that they can count on the facility to do what is says it is going to do and that they can count on knowing exactly what will happen on any given day and any given time. This provides children who come from chaotic backgrounds with a sense of safety and security.

3. Childcare workers will quickly notice that children pay a great deal of attention to the posted schedule and can tell staff what appears there every day.

4. Because the schedule is so important to the children in your care, it is imperative that you follow the schedule to the letter and always get permission from a supervisor before making a change to the schedule.

5. Some staff do not understand the importance of the schedule and offer a variety of reasons for not wanting to follow it. Unfortunately, these reasons have more to do with meeting the needs of that childcare worker than the needs of the children.

6. When a childcare worker does not follow the schedule, there is a major crack in the facility's structure. Children will recognize this and will begin to consciously or unconsciously feel unsafe. If the disregard for the schedule continues, some children may begin to display acting-out behaviors.

7. Scheduled events are not always going to be popular with children; for example, children may not want to get up early on a Saturday, even if they are going to the zoo. Children may try to manipulate staff to add outings, like stopping for ice cream, things that are not on the schedule for that day. In these instances, childcare workers can refer to the schedule as a separate entity, almost like a boss, that dictates what he or she must do while on shift. It is not personal; it is the schedule that the childcare worker is bound to follow.

EXERCISE

Write down five items that regularly appear on the house schedule at your facility. Then after each write about reasons why it appears on the schedule, and finally, add how each enhances the well-being and/ or meets the needs of the children in your care.

1. Item:

   Importance:

2. Item:

   Importance:

3. Item:

   Importance:

4. Item:

   Importance:

5. Item:

   Importance:

Chapter 5

ELEMENTS OF MILIEU THERAPY: MAINTAINING GOOD BOUNDARIES

Five-year-old Carla lived in a small, unkempt apartment with her mother, who was addicted to heroin. Carla watched strangers come and go all day and night to buy or use drugs or pay for sex. She did not know why all these people were always at her house, but to her this was normal. There was no filter on who got in and who did not or who was safe to be around children and who was not. The door was open to anyone. No one told the Carla the difference between good and bad touching or what to do if an adult's behavior was making her uncomfortable. One day her mother was surprised when Child Protective Services came to her apartment. Carla had admitted to a school counselor that her mother's boyfriend had molested her. After an investigation, Carla was removed from her mother's care and placed into a foster home. Carla's mother was shocked and did not believe her own daughter's allegation of molestation, despite medical evidence. It simply did not occur to Carla's mother that her lifestyle might have been putting her daughter's safety at risk.

After being placed in a foster home, Carla's behavior became a problem. Chief among her issues were her boundaries. Carla would walk out of the house and right into the home of a neighbor or try to wander off with strangers at the grocery store. One day her foster mother left Carla and another foster child doing their homework in the dining room while the foster mother made dinner. After fifteen minutes, she came to check on the children and found Carla missing. She frantically searched the house, but Carla was not there. She called a neighbor who came over to watch her other children and got into her car to search for Carla. Finally, she found her ten blocks away standing outside a convenience store talking to a group of teenaged boys. Carla's foster mother asked to have Carla transferred, fearing that she could not keep Carla safe. Carla's social worker agreed that a higher level of care, possibly a residential facility, was warranted. Unfortunately, it not surprising that these serious behaviors were manifesting in Carla. Her mother had role modeled poor boundaries, and Carla mimicked the poor boundaries her mother taught her.

Many of your clients have very poor personal boundaries. Raised in homes with few limits on behavior and interaction with others, many children placed in residential facilities have no idea what healthy boundaries are. Think of the child who will start up a conversation with anyone anywhere–sitting in the doctor's waiting room, at the grocery store, or waiting in line at a movie theater. He hands out personal information to complete strangers matter-of-factly and may even touch or hug the stranger to whom he speaks. You and other staff have worried about his safety. It seems that left on his own he would probably go home with anyone who showed an interest in him. His lack of boundaries may put him in danger one day.

Because of the children's great need for improved personal boundaries as well as the childcare worker's need to maintain professionalism, the success of milieu therapy at your facility depends on all staff having good boundaries in their work with clients. Your personal maintenance of good boundaries is meant to model and teach appropriate boundaries to your clients as well as to ensure that your staff-client relationship remains appropriate and beneficial to all. Practicing good boundaries means that you have healthy personal limits when interacting with clients and coworkers and a clear sense of your job– what it entails and what it does not. It is true that for childcare workers "the inability to establish clear boundaries for themselves is one of the most common areas of difficulty" (Anglin, Denholm, Ferguson, & Pence, 1990, p. 37).

Boundaries become one of the aspects of milieu therapy that is most difficult to teach when training new staff, yet it is one of the most important for staff to learn and internalize while on shift. The root of this difficulty may come from a childcare worker blurring the distinction between personal life and work behavior. In theses cases, talking to a supervisor or some additional training will ameliorate the problem. Many times, however, childcare workers may have inappropriate boundaries themselves, lacking an understanding of what good boundaries mean. If a childcare worker cannot understand or employ good boundaries in his or her own life, he or she will have great difficulty enforcing healthy boundaries in the work environment. Much training may be needed for some childcare workers to understand good boundaries and put them into practice on the job. Some childcare workers may need to seek personal counseling to work through their own poor boundaries to improve job performance, and ultimately their personal lives will benefit as well. Ironically, because of the intangible nature of boundaries, little or no training is given to new staff at most facilities. Trainers have difficulty with the topic and would rather focus on concrete aspects of training. The best training programs for new staff include solid, detail- and example-packed sections on boundaries. When staff have a clear understanding of what it means to have good boundaries as childcare workers, their job performance and retention improves and service to clients becomes better and more professional.

MAINTAINING GOOD BOUNDARIES

Among the most basic aspects of good boundaries is having a clear sense of your role in the milieu as an authority figure in your clients' lives. While you are on shift, clients look to you to have their basic needs met. They depend on you to set limits for their behavior and to uphold the program structure. Once a client has learned that you are a fair, caring authority figure who follows the program structure and meets her needs, she will begin to trust and respect you. She will enjoy interacting with you and will seek you out for advice and counsel. Childcare workers who are unclear about or uncomfortable with their role can actually impede a child's progress in treatment. Let us look at five ways that inappropriate boundaries can manifest in the milieu:

1. Trying to be a friend not an authority figure
2. Sharing personal information
3. Acting outside the scope of practice
4. Practicing favoritism
5. Harboring a rescue fantasy

Friend Not Authority Figure

The emotionally disturbed children in your care need to know that they have adults in charge who are capable and responsible. Many of them have never experienced what it is like to be cared for by adults who are healthy, fair, honest, and consistent. Your clients instinctively long for the environment provided by your facility, and you and your coworkers as a team are filling an authority figure role in the lives of your clients. One of the most basic tasks of residential treatment is to facilitate our children's ability to interact with and accept instruction from authority figures (Trieschman, 1969, p. 89). If a childcare worker does not assume the role of an authority figure, that worker "removes the possibility that the child will learn this from him" (Trieschman, 1969, p. 89).

Many childcare workers new to the field want nothing more than to make friends with the children in their care. They feel much empathy for their clients and the difficult lives they have had. The role of authority figure in their client's life seems cold and distant. They mistakenly think that becoming a friend to the child is more nurturing and comforting. The reality is that their clients usually have plenty of friends, but what they truly need are responsible adults to care for them and set limits for their behavior. Quite commonly child care workers make an error in judgment when they "attempt to become one of the boys. This is common among younger workers . . . who have not yet fully adopted the adult role themselves and who may find it more natural to act as a member of the youngster's peer group" (Trieschman, 1969, p. 89). The childcare worker/friend really operates in conflict with two worlds that will collide the first time he has to give his client/friend consequences for a rule violation. Quite simply, friends do not give friends consequences. When these worlds collide, there will be an explosion that the childcare worker/friend will not be prepared for.

Arlene, a childcare worker at XYZ Home for Girls, embraced her new job with much enthusiasm. At twenty-three she was not much older than the teenaged clients at her work, and she could well remember what it was like being their age. While on shift she enjoyed laughing and talking with the girls. She liked the same kind of music they did and wore the same style of clothing. Being around them felt like being with friends; Arlene loved her job. She and the girls would gossip about cute celebrities and kids at the girls' school. Even though it was against the rules, Arlene secretly brought in one of her trendiest tops and let the girls borrow it. When her "friends" violated minor house rules like swearing, Arlene turned a blind eye.

One day Arlene arrived at work and the girls as usual raced over to greet their "friend." Arlene could scarcely get to the office to put down her purse as the girls clamored for her attention. When she walked back out into the milieu, Arlene saw a girl named Robin slap a younger, more passive girl. Arlene called out to her "friend," asking her to stop "for me." Luckily, Robin did not hit again but instead went to her room. Arlene was shocked. She never imagined that Robin would do such a thing and especially not on Arlene's shift. After all, Robin liked her too much to misbehave while she was working, or so Arlene thought.

Arlene turned and went back into the office where a coworker was doing some charting. After telling the seasoned coworker about what had happened, Arlene was told she would have to complete an incident report as well as give Robin consequences. Arlene wrote the incident report but put off giving consequences until the end of her shift, despite her coworker's advice to do it right away.

Feeling very uncomfortable, Arlene finally approached Robin and told her that she had been given consequences for hitting a peer. Robin exploded in anger and tears. "How could you do this to me?" she cried. "I thought you were my friend, but you're such a bitch." As Robin stormed off to her room, she punched a hole in the hallway wall. It would be weeks before she would speak to Arlene. Arlene was upset and bewildered by the experience and seriously considered quitting her job.

Unfortunately, Robin's reaction, which was so unexpected and puzzling to Arlene, was quite predictable. When an authority figure gives a client restriction, the client may not like it, but she will usually accept the consequence. When someone she thought was her friend gives her restriction, however, it is a betrayal that hurts and confuses. The violent outburst Robin displayed is not an uncommon reaction when a friend gives a friend restriction of privileges. In clients whose emotions are already in turmoil, the confusing message sent by a child-care worker/friend relationship can be quite debilitating. In Robin's case, her behavior continued to decline after her outburst, and she had to be moved to a higher level of care. Arlene's reaction was equally predictable. She was genuinely surprised that her friend would act out on her shift. Here again, the worlds collided when the true and correct nature of the working relationship between the two was revealed.

Arlene talked with her supervisor and received additional training and was able to remain in her position. For weeks after the incident Arlene dreaded going to a job she had once enjoyed, but the support of her supervisor kept her going. Soon she began to better understand and appreciate her role and actually began to love her job again. She never again made the mistake of trying to be a friend to one of her clients and worked hard to keep her boundaries appropriate.

Here again a childcare worker who wants to be friends with her clients may be focusing more on meeting her own needs rather than the needs of her clients. She may want the children to like her and believes that being their friend will make them like her more. As with Arlene, this will eventually backfire. A good supervisor will recognize the problems and be able to provide additional training so that she can get her boundaries and work priorities in alignment.

Sharing Personal Information

Your job as a childcare worker is all about your clients. On shift, the focus must be on your clients and their issues and concerns. When you share personal information with your clients, you have changed the dynamic from being about them to being about you. Not only is this countertherapeutic, but also giving your clients a glimpse into your personal life can have consequences for you personally. For example, if you come to work not feeling up to par because you did not get enough sleep the night before, you must not share this information with your clients. Instead, put your game face on and go about doing your job to the best of your abilities. The information you are not at your best can and will be used against you by your clients if the opportunity arises. If on that day you have to give consequences to a client, she will more than likely complain to your supervisor that you only gave her restriction because you did not get any sleep the night before.

It is a good idea to start with a personal policy that you do not share personal information with your clients, as most employers will require. Personal information includes marital status, dating history, information about your children, details of your past and past behaviors, medical issues, anecdotes about your life outside of work, and so on. In your work with children, you will find

> If we are to maintain any sense of self-integrity it is essential that in each encounter, we determine how much we are prepared to share at any particular time with any particular person. A failure to establish such personal "boundaries" can have devastating personal and interpersonal consequences. It should be emphasized that a commitment to pursue a pathway of complete self-disclosure is a very serious decision to be made and agreed upon by two people who intend to experience a state of intimacy. Within the context of the practitioner-child relationship this goal is considered to be both impossible and undesirable. (Anglin, et al., p. 28)

Staff sharing personal information with clients does not enhance good practice in the milieu. Instead, it may create an artificially intimate bond with clients that may eventually begin to feel like or become a bond of friendship rather than authority figure-child. If you begin to share personal information with your clients, you run the risk of the relationship's crossing over into a friendship. As you become more and more comfortable with sharing about yourself with a client, your role as an authority figure becomes increasingly blurred. If you are to keep your relationship on a functional, professional level, sharing of personal information will only undermine your effectiveness as a child-care worker.

As you may already have noticed, your clients are very interested in you. They probably have asked you a litany of personal questions. Of particular interest to them are your age and your love life. Your clients will want to know if you are married or if you have a girlfriend or boyfriend. Many times, new childcare workers will answer those questions because they do not want to be rude, but the well-trained staff will deflect the question and put the focus back onto the client. Here are some examples of how you could respond without "being rude":

1. Oh, you don't want to hear about me. I'm pretty boring. Let's talk about you.
2. I'm sorry, but I don't really feel comfortable talking about that, but didn't you just say you liked going to the beach?

3. I don't really talk about stuff like that when I'm working. Hey, do you like that song that's playing?

As the situation presents itself you will be able to choose the type of response that works with your personality and fits the situation. Remember, the idea is always to get the focus off you and back on the client. If you wear a wedding ring, the children will, of course, notice. If they ask are you married, you can simply say yes, change the subject, and leave it at that. There is no point in denying or avoiding the obvious. Also, women who are pregnant will not be able to deny when children ask; however, your clients do not need to know the particulars such as sex of the child, due date, or the identity of the father. The less said about your pregnancy while interacting with your clients the better for you and for them.

Some childcare workers have difficulty with not sharing personal lives with their clients. A childcare worker may think that sharing the fact that he is in drug or alcohol recovery with his thirteen-year-old client will help a young man struggling with his own issues of addiction. Another staff member may believe that telling her twelve-year-old client that she was molested as a child too can make the young girl see that she is not alone and someone understands what she is going through. Yet another staff member feels that letting her clients know that she too grew up in a group home would help them relate to her better. None of these approaches is a good idea because sharing that personal information:

1. Does not make the child feel more secure in the milieu or enhance your practice as a milieu counselor
2. May make the child become overly concerned for your well-being
3. Removes the focus from the child's issues and concerns
4. Is most likely offered through other neutral sources

A childcare worker must represent a strong, consistent authority figure who responds to and fills a child's needs. Perhaps for the first time in their lives, the children in your care feel protected and cared for by adults in their lives. When deciding whether or not to share personal information, ask yourself, "Will my client's knowing this make him feel more secure? Will sharing the information make me a better childcare worker?"

When deciding to share or not to share personal information, use the test of whether the information is available through neutral sources first. If you are thinking of sharing that you are a molestation survivor, this test will reveal that there is plenty of information and support available through neutral sources. There are support groups for molestation survivors and counseling programs designed specifically for them. Most definitely your client is already working on these issues with the psychologist she sees through your residential program. If you feel that the child needs more support and is not attending any groups or counseling programs, suggest to your supervisor that doing so might be a good idea. Your supervisor will have a better grasp of the history of the client and will probably consult with other professionals at the facility based upon your suggestion. In the end, the professional help will be better than your sharing of your personal information.

Oftentimes, the sharing of personal information can make the child feel less secure. Let us look at an example. Harold, a childcare worker at Alvin's Group Home, shared his history of drug and alcohol recovery with his client Timmy, who at thirteen struggled with his own chemical dependency issues. Although Harold told Timmy for "all the right reasons," the situation did not turn out the way Harold had envisioned. Timmy began to act out while Harold was on shift when in the past he had been a model client. In addition, Timmy became withdrawn while Harold was on shift and began to avoid all interactions with him.

Why did this happen? Harold had been Timmy's favorite and most respected staff person. He looked up to Harold and always followed his directives, knowing that he could count on Harold to be consistent and fair. The news that Harold was a drug addict hit Timmy hard. He immediately flashed to his earlier years growing up with a mother who abused drugs. As a pang of fear rose in his stomach, Timmy wondered if Harold would be okay, if he would start using drugs again, and if he could rely on Harold as he had for anything.

Would it be the same with Harold? Young Timmy simply could not process, understand, or reconcile the information that Harold, a trusted adult, had given him. As a defense to protect himself, Timmy backed away from Harold completely and rarely spoke to him after the day Harold took the focus off Timmy and put it on to himself.

Personal information you share with clients may cause your clients to become concerned for your well-being. Once again, as clients become worried about you, the focus is off of themselves and the important work they need to do to heal themselves. As they worry about you, they may underperform at school, in the facility, and in therapy. As we saw with Timmy, Harold's disclosure of his substance abuse history caused the boy to become concerned about Harold's health and safety to the exclusion of the child's own therapeutic concerns. In addition, the disclosure created fear and anxiety in the boy because Timmy worried about Harold's ability to continue to stay well and be there for him.

As you share personal information with your clients, you become the focus of your work with them, and their concerns, responsibilities, and issues take a back seat. While on shift you must be focused on your clients' lives and talk about what concerns them—not what concerns you. A nurse does not come to work and talk to her sick patient about the troubles she is having with her boyfriend. She talks about what is going on with that patient. So you must focus your attention on your clients and leave your own baggage at the door.

Sometimes even sharing benign or positive information with clients can cause clients to absorb your personal information and make comparisons with their own lives. Three girls living in a group home were placed into the same classroom for emotionally disturbed students at a local high school. The teacher, whom they initially liked, talked frequently about her two daughters. She would go on about how much fun they had as a family and brag about her daughters' looks and achievements. One of the group home girls began to act out in the classroom and on more than one occasion had to be sent home. The other two girls stopped wanting to go to school and often came home from school looking depressed. Finally, one of the girls told a childcare worker that the teacher's talk about her idyllic family life caused them to reflect upon their own fractured families. The result was the girls began to feel more frustrated and depressed about their own circumstances.

The fact is, you cannot predict how a client will react to any personal disclosure, no matter how well-intentioned. Your clients are emotionally disturbed, and past traumas and current issues can be triggered or created by even the most seemingly inconsequential personal information you share with them. There is no better way to avoid this than keeping the focus on them and off yourself at all times. This even includes personal discussions you have with coworkers while on shift. You may think that your clients are not listening or cannot hear you, but do not be fooled. Children have amazing hearing abilities when it comes to what you might consider a private conversation with a coworker. While on the job, it is best not to talk about your personal life at all. If you become friendly with a coworker and would like to have a personal conversation with him or her, have that conversation outside of work.

Finally, your clients are already receiving counsel and education on a wide variety of subjects via classes, therapy sessions, and special programs. Clients with substance abuse issues are attending groups on addiction. Children who have been molested or are domestic violence victims are in special groups and individual and family therapy. The knowledge they receive comes from neutral sources and has just as much impact and import as anything you could disclose to them. When they receive the information in this way, clients do not have to worry about anyone in their therapeutic environment and have only to apply what they have learned to themselves.

There are rare occasions when sharing your experience with a client can be of benefit; however, the information must be benign, nonspecific, and not intensely personal. For example, Carol's client Maria complained to her that she was being bullied at school. Carol listened quietly to Maria as she talked about the teasing she endured. After awhile, Carol shared with Maria that she, too, had been bullied at school and understood what it felt like. She then went on to assure Maria that the bullying was only temporary and would pass. She also told Maria that the bullies themselves were not children who felt good about themselves because a happy person would not think of making someone else feel bad to make themselves feel good. She offered to have someone from the group home call her teacher to discuss the situation. Then Carol immediately shifted the attention back to Maria, reassuring her that she was a lovely young lady with many talents and abilities unique to her. Maria left the conversation feeling better about herself and the bullying.

Carol handled the situation beautifully. She listened and then shared in as few words as possible an episode from her own life that was not intensely personal or traumatic. She offered insight and suggested ways to assist Maria by getting school personnel to help. Most importantly, she turned the conversation back to Maria as she attempted to boost her client's self-esteem in the face of the teasing.

As you work in this field and gain experience, you will learn to differentiate when it is appropriate to share personal information and when it is not. However, early on in your career it may not be so easy to recognize. Better to refrain from sharing personal information, or if you feel strongly that disclosing would be appropriate, discuss the matter with your supervisor before taking action.

Acting Outside of Your Scope of Practice

Having good boundaries as a childcare worker means you understand your job and what it entails as well as what it does not entail. Overall, your job description is your guide to what duties are involved with your work on shift. During your initial training, your duties were carefully explained to you. If you do not understand your job duties and the limits of your responsibilities and authority, you need to get clarification from your supervisor as soon as possible.

Although in some ways childcare workers fulfill a "parental role" for clients in the milieu, many of the decisions and choices a parent would make are outside of your scope of practice because you are not the child's parent. You are not a legal guardian and cannot make some of the decisions a parent or legal guardian could make. Because you are not the child's legal guardian, you cannot act as one in many situations, particularly when medical issues are involved. For example, you might decide to give your own teenaged son an extra ibuprophen when he gets a migraine, but you simply have no authority to do this with one of your clients. Only a doctor can authorize increasing the dosage, even for an over-the-counter medication. If you do not follow package instructions, you are acting as a doctor, which is outside of your scope of practice.

Many times children who have been abused have many somatic complaints. They report aches and pains, sometimes believe they are seriously injured after a minor mishap, and at times will fear they suffer from a serious disease. In these instances the childcare worker cannot say what he might to his own child. Whereas a parent might tell her child that she is okay and is just imagining that the benign bump on her arm is cancer when it really looks like a pimple, you cannot dismiss the child's report and must have the child seen by a doctor. A medical professional must check every health-related complaint.

Even in situations where it seems fairly believable that nothing is truly wrong with a client, a medical doctor must examine and make a diagnosis. One evening a thirteen-year-old girl who lived at a residential treatment center began to cry and scream and hold her stomach. Staff on duty knew exactly what was happening because the same thing happened the week before: the girl had been taken to the emergency room in an ambulance, a battery of tests was conducted, and no medical problem was found. A follow-up examination with her primary care physician yielded the same results, but here it was a week later and the girl was experiencing the same symptoms. When the child complained of pain that night, staff talked to the client, who told them she wanted to go to the emergency room. When asked if she would be able to ride in the van to the hospital, she said no she could not even walk to the van the pain was so great. Staff were reluctant to call an ambulance after what had happened last week. One staff said, "If she were my kid, I'd tell her to have a cup of tea and relax because she had already been checked and nothing was wrong." Although staff knew the procedure, they still were reluctant to act and decided to call their supervisor. Of course, the supervisor told them to call the ambulance immediately, saying that no one was qualified to diagnose a medical condition except a doctor. He added that not being the child's legal guardians, the childcare workers on shift had no right or authority to deny the child's request for a doctor based on the events of the prior week. "What if this time her appendix was ready to burst?" the supervisor said. "Not being trained medical professionals you have no way of knowing. We must leave that to a doctor."

A good rule of thumb for remembering scope of practice is this: if the task requires a licensed or certified professional and you do not possess that license or certification, you should not perform that task for your clients. This includes doing a clients hair or nails, because a licensed beautician must do these tasks. Especially when working with teenaged girls, the issue of hair and makeup will almost inevitably come up. A girl may ask you if you will do her hair in a French braid, and you may think there would be little harm in that. However, the touch and intimacy of doing her hair may be misinterpreted, particularly if she has been molested. This could change your relationship with that client because a boundary has been blurred. Better to have a disinterested licensed beautician perform the service. Oftentimes, teenaged girls will want to dye their hair and may ask you to help them apply a kit that was purchased at the drugstore. You simply do not have the expertise to do this. If the child is injured in some way, such as her scalp being burned or irritated, you will be held accountable and your job may be put in jeopardy.

In the same way, you cannot relabel or repackage medications because you are not a licensed pharmacist. You simply are not qualified to override the pharmacist's and doctor's instruction even if you have personal experience with the medication, and incidentally, this practice is against the law and with good reason.

Practicing Favoritism

Almost everyone can remember a teacher, coach, or camp counselor who picked out one or two children who became their pets. The "chosen ones" received all kinds of praise and special privileges, and other classmates were frequently unfavorably compared to them. As you watched, your self-esteem dropped daily. You may have started to dislike going to school or even experienced school anxiety symptoms, such as stomach upset, to avoid attending school. In the face of the daily rejection, your grades may have begun to suffer.

As hard as that experience was for you and your fellow classmates, you try to imagine what it would feel like for a client in your care. Your clients have been abused, abandoned, or neglected by their parents or caregivers. They may have moved from placement to placement over a period of just a few years. Most have very little self-esteem and a lot of confusion and anger. Being rejected by yet another adult reinforces the message that adults cannot be trusted to treat others fairly. The rejection can also reinjure an already hurting child by opening old wounds from the child's past that have yet to fully heal. When working with your clients, it is imperative that you remain fair and impartial in your contact with each in the milieu. You do not want to repeat the cycle of rejection and abandonment and reinjure the children in your care. If you show favoritism for one client over another, you risk harming the client.

Make no mistake; your clients are on the lookout for any sign of favoritism and will heartily complain about it in most instances. Perhaps this is because they are more accustomed to being treated unfairly. They have, after all, been let down by the most important adults in their lives. So one of the most common complaints that supervisors will hear from children is that a childcare worker is showing favoritism to another child. Fortunately most of the time the complaints are not warranted. Unfortunately, in the instances where favoritism is really occurring, a rejected child may not have the desire or confidence to speak up for himself and may begin to act out in self-destructive ways.

When you show favoritism, you are not practicing good boundaries because you have shifted the focus of your work from meeting the needs of your clients. Meeting the needs of your clients means that each child is treated fairly and equally. Showing preference for one child and allowing her special privileges or looking the other way when she breaks a rule does not meet the needs of your clients. In fact, your actions of favoritism could quickly throw the milieu into upheaval as children begin to act out their frustration, anger, and hurt. If you are treating one client better than the others, you need to take a hard look at your motives. Are you hoping he will want you as a friend? Are you acting out a past trauma of your own and rewriting the ending? You need to discuss the issue with your supervisor, who may recommend some counseling to help you work through whatever is motivating you to show favoritism to a particular client. Indeed, showing favoritism most often indicates that you are acting in a way that will get your need for attention met while ignoring the needs of the group of children with whom you work.

Of course, you are only human and are not going to like every client equally. One child may remind you of a beloved niece or nephew or even your own son or daughter. Another may bring to mind memories of yourself at that age. Other clients may be oppositional, angry, and difficult to engage in any activity. Even though some clients are much easier to like than others, you must never allow anything but equal regard and treatment to be seen by all of your clients. At the group home for girls where she worked, childcare worker Janine was excited that a new boy was about to arrive for intake. She loved helping the children learn about their new home and learn the ropes of the program. When the young red-haired boy came through the door,

Janine almost gasped. He looked exactly like a boy who bullied her when she was about the same age. To make matters worse, his behaviors matched her bully's behaviors so closely it was almost eerie. He started right off bullying the other boys and even staff. At a staff meeting, she and her colleagues discussed strategies for dealing with his behavior. Janine sat quietly during the meeting. Ashamed to admit it, she really disliked that child. She felt a lot of empathy for the children being bullied. On shift she had to fight the instinct to pile extra restriction of privileges on the boy while being extra considerate and nice to the other children. She could so understand their suffering, but her training had told her that she needed to treat them all equally. After a couple of weeks she discussed the matter with her supervisor, who praised her efforts to remain fair and equal. Her supervisor suggested that Janine journal about the past victimization by the bully in her life in order to work through her feelings. Janine followed her advice and found the exercise extremely useful. After a few days of journaling, she discovered that she could approach the situation at work without attaching her past baggage to the young bully. It took awhile but thanks to the efforts of Janine and the staff at her program, the boy's bullying began to sharply diminish. After all was said and done, Janine found him to be a strong-willed and determined boy who appeared to have a bright future ahead.

Rescue Fantasy

Unfortunately, many people interested in fulfilling their own needs choose to work with at-risk children. Poor boundaries may be a symptom of a deeper issue that some adults, even the highly educated, are attempting to work out through their clients. Many adults have a rescue fantasy, a need to save another person coupled with a belief that they are the only one who will be able to fix that person's life. A rescue fantasy is really a more serious form of favoritism in which a client is not only favored but also seen as needing to be saved by the rescuer. In the rescuer's mind, no one else can "save" the child—not the other childcare workers, county workers, program social worker, or program psychologist. Taken to the extreme, the rescuer may begin to believe that he is the only one who knows what is right for a particular client.

Because many enter your field with tremendous heart and empathy for children, some will become fixated on doing whatever they have to do to "save" one or more children in their care. As we have seen, favoritism can cause reinjury to other children in care. As a more extreme version of favoritism, a rescue fantasy can cause the same effects for the other children. However, a rescue fantasy can also cause harmful effects for the child who is the object of a childcare worker's rescue fantasy. Two significant risks are involved: (1) The child's treatment will be disrupted or undermined, or (2) the rescuing childcare worker will quickly burnout under the pressure, leaving the child feeling abandoned and alone. When a childcare worker tries to rescue a client, she will do anything and everything to save that child. She forgets that she is part of a team and ignores the fact that her role on the team is critical to her client's successes. Instead, she tries to do the work of everyone on the treatment team. The rescuer creates an artificial bond with the client, who many times becomes dependent on her. The client's relationships with other staff suffer. She becomes less invested in therapy, abandons plans for her future, such as transitional housing or even reunification with family; and puts all of her hope in the hands of her rescuer. Many times a rescuer will invite his client to come live with him because the rescuer often reasons that is the best way to save him. Unfortunately, the rescuer's plans are usually not well-thought-out, and the realization of the fantasy is often disappointing. The clients are often the ones who suffer, having been cut off from the many resources that surrounded them before the rescuers appeared. As pointed out in the book *The Other 24 Hours,*

> We cannot promise to be all things to a child unless that child is our own. The worker who selects a particular child and showers him with gifts, special privileges, or constant attention is promising a parental relationship he will be unable to sustain. Not only do other children and staff resent such favoritism, but sometimes the child will avoid the adult to avoid being labeled as somebody's pet. (Trieschman, 1969, p. 90)

More likely, however, a needy, abused child will seek out and enjoy the attentions of the worker with a rescue fantasy. The danger is that when the rescuing worker moves on, for whatever reason, the child will experience another abandonment. The outcome for the child is that he or she will be reinjured by the staff member's rescue fantasy.

Burnout is a significant risk for those who harbor a rescue fantasy. Because rescuers feel great pressure to be everything to their client, they quickly become overwhelmed. The needs of the children in residential treatment are significant; it truly takes a full staff of professionals and paraprofessionals to provide the comprehensive treatment they require. Those who attempt to be everything to a client will become overburdened. They may neglect their own health and well-being and show signs and symptoms of stress and anxiety. If the client they are trying to rescue fails at their facility, the rescuers may experience significant guilt and feelings of inadequacy. Overwhelmed and exhausted, the rescuers may not be able to continue their employment, or their rescue fantasy may be viewed as such a problem that they may lose their job.

If you find yourself wanting to rescue your clients, you should talk to your supervisor immediately. She or he will be able to offer advice and may even suggest some counseling to help you deal with the issue. Your supervisor will be able to discuss specifics of the clients with whom you work and point out where your desire to save is flawed.

You will avoid any desire to rescue if you understand the following principles about your work:

1. Your clients have many complex issues and circumstances requiring a treatment team made up of professionals and paraprofessionals as well as family and other concerned individuals.
2. No one person can handle the complexities of any client's case, just as no one perspective adequately fulfills any client's many needs.
3. The treatment that any client receives at your facility is just a segment of the treatment a client received before arriving and will likely need and hopefully receive after leaving your facility.
4. For many children, no one treatment team or treatment facility is the answer for all of their problems.

Let us take a look at each of these points in detail. The result will be an increased understanding of your role and your facility's role in the treatment of each child that comes to your facility.

The Need for a Team

The children in your care have a variety of difficult and complex issues and a variety of circumstances that have placed them into residential care. A child may have an eating disorder, substance abuse issues, and impulse control. He may have learning disorders that require special classes, constant monitoring, and tutoring. His family may be dysfunctiona, yet still loving and eager to remain in the child's life. Family counseling may be on going to reunite the child with his family. Children in residential care may have several psychological diagnoses and traits that often make their behavior unpredictable and even dangerous to themselves or to others. Remember many of these children have been placed in residential care because they could not be maintained in traditional family foster homes and were referred to residential care because they needed a higher level of care, structure, and supervision. To address the child's many issues a team of professional and paraprofessionals is essential.

The children at your facility will need a team consisting of the following: milieu therapists, program social worker, psychologist, family therapist, psychiatrist, county social worker, court-appointed special advocate, and family members. As we have discussed, a team of milieu therapists/childcare workers who are fair and consistent is of the utmost importance to the treatment of children in residential care. Childcare workers provide a safe, comforting environment for the children while enforcing structure and setting limits. They also are role models for positive and appropriate behavior while helping children learn that adults can be trusted and even fun to be around. The program social worker acts as the facility's case manager for each child and is responsible for a variety of important functions of the treatment facility. She or he oversees the child's treatment, networks with other members of the child's treatment team to keep them apprised of the child's progress, plans and schedules activities for the children that encompass a variety of interests, works with staff and each child to determine treatment goals, and tracks the progress toward each goal. Above all, the program social worker is an advocate for each client, making sure that the child's needs large and small are met, including the child's needs in the future. For example, if a client needs a individualized education program to determine if she needs additional assistance at school so that her learning goals can be met, the program social worker must recognize that need, call for the process to begin, and follow it to its conclusion. The program's psychologist is an important part of the team, providing counseling for the many deep-rooted issues that trouble the abused children in residential care. Because many of the children in residential care are on one or more medications to control moods or anxiety or to decrease depression, to name a few symptoms, a psychiatrist is an essential team member who monitors the psychotropic medications the children are prescribed. Perhaps the most important member of the team is the child's county worker, who may have been assigned to the child's case for a number of years and therefore has a unique knowledge of the child and his family and history. The county worker may also have the child's siblings on her caseload as well. It is the county worker who directs the child's case overall and relies on the facility to provide treatment and progress updates.

Family members are also an important part of a child's treatment team and must be included in decision making and planning. It is imperative that each child has a network of people who love and care for him or her. In spite of history, illness, or mistakes, family members are most often the ones who will be there for children for the rest of their lives. They are the ones to whom children will turn when they are in need as children or as adults. A good treatment team will include as many family members who are willing and able to assist.

Although the preceding section gives a good understanding of the number and types of people that are, and must be, involved in each child's treatment team, the descriptions only scratch the surface of the many functions and responsibilities of each team member. If it takes a village to raise a "normal" child, it can be said that it takes a city to raise, treat and care for a child in residential treatment.

In most cases, the behaviors that were manifested in foster homes or their family homes will reappear should they go into a rescuer's home. You will notice with many children coming into a new facility that there is a "honeymoon" period when children are on on their best behavior. After a period of time, the true behaviors of the child begin to surface. This phenomenon is likely to manifest in the rescuer's dealing with the child while the child is in placement and certainly after a period of time in the rescuer's home. It is highly unlikely that the rescuer will be able to provide the level of service the child needs, no matter how agreeable the child appears in the rescuer's interactions with him or her.

One Person Cannot Be Everything

Because of all of your clients' issues, no one person can handle the complexities of any client's case, just as no one perspective adequately fulfills any client's many needs. As you can see, there are many professionals and paraprofessionals involved in the maintenance of each of your client's cases. It would be extremely difficult for one person to manage all of the different services that a client needs. The rescuer may think he can take care of them, but he will find in actual practice that the child's case is overwhelmingly difficult to handle on his own. In addition, each of the professionals involved brings a different perspective based upon his or her education and experience. Although the rescuer may be able to bring in outside services to assist, it would be very hard to match the level of services and perspectives that are offered and implemented in the residential setting. As a result, the child's psychological, emotional, social, and physical well-being will begin to suffer.

Your Facility is Just a Piece of the Sum Total of Care and Treatment

The treatment that any client receives at your facility is just a segment of the treatment a client received before arriving and will likely need and hopefully receive after leaving your facility. Consider your client's treatment as represented by a pie shape. The treatment the child receives at your facility is just one of the pieces of that pie. Treatment received at previous facilities, outpatient clinics, special programs and classes, and work with different therapists form other pieces of the pie. The rest of the pieces of the pie are made of up the facilities and other therapeutic interventions she will receive in the future. Children who have been abused, molested, abandoned, and/or neglected are not "fixed" by a single person or program. Placements where the children were prior to arriving at yours did their part; your facility will do its part. Unfortunately, many will likely need additional services after they leave your facility and on into their adulthoods.

Brian had been in four different facilities before he reached Mark's group home for boys. During the next staff meeting after Brian's intake, Mark, who was the program social worker, gave the staff of child-care workers a brief synopsis of Brian's history. He told them that when Brian first came into the foster care system he lived for two years in the foster home of an older couple who cared for him as their own and gave him lots of love and attention after raising their own children. When the wife was tragically killed in a car accident, the husband was no longer able to care for Brian, so Brian was placed in a series of foster homes, where his behavior became increasingly difficult. Finally, at one of the foster homes where he felt especially close to the foster parent, Brian disclosed that he had been molested by his mother's boyfriend prior to being removed from his mother's care. Although the foster parent tried to get services for Brian, his county worker soon placed him into a residential treatment facility that specialized in working with boys who had been molested. After spending a year in that facility, Brian was old enough and ready to move to Mark's facility, which specialized in working with older boys who were preparing for independent living. Mark pointed out to the staff how each of the key placements had fulfilled a specific purpose in Brian's continuing treatment and care. The first foster home smoothed his transition out of home care by providing him with love and support. At the home where he disclosed his molestation, he was given a trusting, safe environment where he could open up about his history and open the door to healing. The residential facility that handled molested children helped him handle the scars that had been left by his victimization. Now it was time for Mark to fill in its piece of the pie of Brian's treatment: teaching him the independent living skills he would need to survive in the future.

No Simple Answers

For many children, no one treatment team or treatment facility is the answer for all of their problems. Whereas your facility may be especially good at the time for helping a client with a specific issue, another facility may be the perfect fit to help in other areas. As we have seen, the work done at your facility may only assist with a small segment of the client's treatment needs. Another facility may help with another area where the child needs intervention. For example, a previous facility might have assisted a client with substance abuse or molestation issues, and your facility might help with independent living skills, such as graduating from high school and preparing for employment as an adult. That same child will most likely need services such as counseling and social work advocacy for support when he or she reaches the age of eighteen. In most states, there are many programs and services to help these boys and girls who are exiting the foster care system, including continuation of health care benefits. Some states are currently considering raising the age of dependency to twenty-one, meaning that children could remain in foster care until they reach that age.

When you think of your self as part of a much-needed and well-functioning team, your boundaries in this regard are strong and clear. When you further consider that the work your team is doing right now is just a piece of a larger pie that represents your client's total treatment picture, you gain an even better perspective. As you interact with your clients, you may become invested in them and want to help as much as you can. Step back and remember that you are part of that team, and it is the team as a whole that gets the work done for the client's best interests. Remember that you work, and the many daily interactions you have with your client as a milieu therapist are very important. By doing your part as a milieu therapist, you will be assisting your clients in very important ways, and doing what they need at that time and place in the complete perspective of their treatment and move toward a more healthy adulthood.

CHAPTER 5 REVIEW

1. The success of milieu therapy at any facility depends on all staff members having good boundaries in their work with children.

2. Good boundaries mean that a childcare worker has set healthy personal limits when interacting with children and coworkers and has a clear sense of his or her job, what it entails and what it does not, and an understanding of his or her role as an authority figure for the children in care.

3. Inappropriate boundaries can happen in the milieu when a childcare worker tries to be a friend and not an authority figure.

Children in care do not need more friends. They do need reliable, safe, authority figures to assist them and help meet their needs. The "friend not authority figure" relationship crumbles the first time the childcare worker has to give a "friend" consequences.

4. Another way poor boundaries are seen in the milieu happens when childcare workers share personal information with the children in their care. Childcare workers should limit the sharing of information about themselves with children. While on shift, it is about the children, not the childcare worker. When a childcare worker shares personal information, the focus can quickly shift to being about the childcare worker and not the child.

5. Practicing favoritism shows inappropriate boundaries and can cause a breakdown in the structure of a facility. Oftentimes, this breakdown can have serious consequences for children, who may be reinjured by the preferential treatment of another child.

6. Childcare workers' understanding of their job and what it entails as well as what it does not is critical to maintaining good boundaries. In short, childcare workers should never provide any service to a child in care that would require the services of a licensed professional.

7. One of the most potentially difficult ways poor boundaries can be manifested in the milieu is when a childcare worker has a rescue fantasy. A childcare worker with a rescue fantasy feels that he and only he can "save" a particular child. In most instances, a childcare worker with a rescue fantasy will require counseling to determine the reasons behind her compulsion.

8. To avoid problems with boundaries, it is important for childcare workers to remember that they are part of a team that includes not only people at the facility but also people from the county, family and friends of the child, and other advocates. Furthermore, the treatment that a child receives at your facility is only one segment of the treatment that child has likely already re -

ceived and will receive in the future. No one person is equipped to handle all the nuances and complexities of the cases of the children who are placed in residential care.

EXERCISES

Write down three questions that children in your care have asked you about yourself and how you have redirected the questions in order to turn the focus back on your client.

1. Question:

   Response:

2. Question:

   Response:

3. Question:

   Response:

Write about a time when you or a friend was the victim of an authority figure's practicing favoritism. Describe the situation and how it made you or your friend feel.

Were you surprised by your reaction to this exercise? If so, explain.

Write down five reasons why a childcare worker might have a rescue fantasy.

1.

2.

3.

4.

5.

Chapter 6

ELEMENTS OF MILIEU THERAPY:
SETTING LIMITS

In the dysfunctional homes from which your clients came, there was probably little happening to teach them good behavior and help them improve bad behavior. On the contrary, right and wrong were probably two very blurred concepts in their minds. A mentally ill mother may laugh hysterically one day when her young child runs around the motel room knocking an overflowing ashtray onto the carpet. When the child knocks over the same ashtray the next day, she may become very angry, yell at the child, and whip him with a leather belt until welts appear on his skin.

Many of your clients grew up with very little attention from their adult caregivers. Most likely the only attention they received was negative attention for bad behavior. The message they got loud and clear was that the way to get mother's attention is to misbehave. In their minds, negative attention was better than no attention. Whereas children growing up in functioning homes seek out their parents' praise, the children in your care behaved badly to get the only real attention they could from their parents. It is no surprise that you will see a lot of inappropriate behavior coming from the clients placed at your facility. The children will continue to repeat the negative attention-seeking behaviors that they learned before they entered placement, trying to get attention from you in the same way they learned to get attention from their parents.

Before they were placed outside of their homes, your clients most likely were rarely rewarded, praised, or encouraged when they exhibited good behavior or accomplishments. As a result, the children felt they were not valued or appreciated. They learned that hard work at school or elsewhere did not really earn much of anything, whereas bad behavior got everyone paying attention. Soon they were channeled away from efforts to achieve in any arena. Because they were not motivated to achieve, they soon began to experience failure after failure in school and other settings. As a result, their self-esteem began to suffer. You will find that the children in your care may place little or no value on good behavior and suffer from low self-esteem. Aaron was only nine years old when he entered residential care. He had been in several foster homes and had failed in each. Foster parents became frustrated because, despite their best efforts, they could not encourage him to do well in any arena. The last pair of foster parents enrolled him in karate classes, hoping the discipline and opportunity to achieve would help him. Instead, Aaron barely participated in the classes and then became embarrassed that he was not doing as well as the other students. In school it was the same; he would put forth little or no effort to excel in his classes. When he came home from school, he told his parents that he did not like himself and wished he would just die. A social worker was called in and Aaron was moved to a group home where he could receive more intensive treatment services. The social worker told his saddened foster parents that Aaron suffered from very low self-esteem, most likely from the neglect he received from his biological mother, who suffered from a mental illness. She assured them he would get the help he needed in residential care, where trained people would work with him twenty-four hours a day every day.

To survive in extremely dysfunctional homes, children learn to manipulate to get their needs met. In an existence lacking rules or structure, resilient kids learn to get what they need from neglectful parents or other adults in dysfunctional ways. They bargain and bribe, lie and cheat, misbehave and have tantrums, and do not take no for an answer often. Some children develop passive-aggressive behaviors. Because this is engrained behavior, you will see a lot of these manipulative behaviors in your clients. In placement, they use the behaviors they have learned and often the only behaviors they know. These manipulative behaviors are familiar and comfortable for them. Children will try to manipulate the staff the same way they manipulated their earlier caregivers.

Sylvia was a precocious ten year old who had learned to lie to cover for her alcoholic mother. When the school asked why she was wearing dirty clothes to school, she would tell them what her mother had told her to say—the washing machine was broken and a new one was being delivered in a few days. Neighbors often fed her when she went hungry, and Sylvia would always protect her mother. "My mom's not a good cook at all," she would tell them with a cute smile. "Your food is so much better." After missing school for more than a week because her mother was ill with alcohol poisoning, Sylvia told her teacher that she had gone on a trip with her mother to visit family, which her mother's note to the school confirmed. Eventually, the case was referred several times to child protective services, and Sylvia was placed in a residential shelter while awaiting placement. From the moment she arrived, Sylvia lied even when the truth would do. She told grand stories about her life and her family, which the staff knew were untrue. Her peers also knew that Sylvia was lying. She also lied in instances in which peers were blamed for her behavior. Sylvia's peer relationships were poor. The other girls began to shun her. Her pattern of lying continued in subsequent facilities and at school, making life very difficult for Sylvia. It would take more than a year of intervention before she began to see what effect this behavior was having and would have on her life. Only then was she ready to begin the path to changing her behavior.

Children instinctively look to their parents or guardians to care for them, protect them, and make sure their basic needs are met. Unfortunately, in many cases the adults in your clients' lives failed to do these things. They did not adequately supervise and keep their children safe, too often resulting in sexual abuse. Domestic violence may have occurred in their homes, and the child may have been a victim or may have observed others being harmed. Neglected and abused children quickly learn they cannot count on their parents to provide them with shelter, food, clothing, or a safe environment in which to live. In short, the adult authority figures let their children down.

As a result, many children who come from neglectful and abusive backgrounds develop oppositional defiant disorder, which means they do not trust or respect authority figures. Who can blame them? Unfortunately, children with oppositional defiant disorder are in danger of progressing to the more serious diagnoses of conduct disorder or antisocial personality disorder. Kendra was placed at a facility for girls. She was removed from her family home after repeated instances of domestic violence between her parents resulted in their arrests. Arriving at the facility, she immediately let it be known that she did not have to listen to staff and would do whatever she pleased. Clearly, Kendra had learned not to respect authority figures because of her parent's actions. It took many months of interactions with childcare workers, therapy with her psychologist, and attending a group for survivors of domestic violence before she began to trust staff and look to them to meet her needs and set limits for her behavior. For her it was a big step toward a healthy adulthood.

Somehow the children in your care learned to survive in very difficult environments when they were very young. They did so by developing maladaptive behaviors, which essentially means they developed inappropriate behaviors such as manipulation, lying, or stealing in response to their dysfunctional home environments. Although these behaviors served them at home, these same behaviors will cause problems in other places where normalcy prevails. At school, in a residential facility, and later in a work environment, their maladaptive behaviors will not be accepted. As they grow and form relationships with others, their maladaptive behaviors will be problematic and result in many broken or strained relationships. Although your clients actually might deserve praise for developing behaviors that helped them to survive, the time has come to work on replacing them with appropriate behavioral responses. Their future success and happiness depends on it.

In a home where the mother was always high on heroin, three-year-old Leon learned that throwing the loudest tantrum he could muster was the only way to get her attention. As Leon grew up and reached his teen years, the maladaptive tantrum behavior continued, fueled by adolescent angst and his anger at being placed in the system for many years while his mother could not stay off drugs. Whenever Leon did not get his way, he would launch into a loud, angry tirade filled with expletives. No matter how small the disappointment, his response contained the same histrionic vehemence. At six foot two inches, Leon was quite intimidating. He experienced several failed placements because of this behavior. Finally, after working diligently in anger management therapy, Leon was able to control his tantrums, and when he turned sixteen he was able to hold a job for more than a year. He was well-liked and respected by his coworkers and supervisor.

The negative behavior exhibited by your clients is not a reflection on you or your program, peers, or other staff. In many cases, the children in your care simply do not understand the difference between appropriate and inappropriate behavior. Dr. Morris Fritz Mayer writes, "Disobediences and defiance are not accidental. They often stem from impulses not within a child's conscious control" (Mayer, 1958, p. 136). Children in residential care act out because they are depressed, angry or anxious, and they continue to employ the same maladaptive behaviors that worked for them before they were removed from their homes. A childcare worker should never take a child's difficult behavior personally. It is simply not personal. The children cannot help but behave the way they learned to behave in their dysfunctional homes.

SETTING LIMITS FOR BEHAVIOR IN THE MILIEU

Among the most important work done in the milieu is teaching the difference between appropriate and inappropriate behavior through your facility's system of reward and consequence. It is imperative that you set limits for inappropriate behaviors, encourage appropriate behaviors, and help build healthy self-esteem. In his book *No Such Thing as a Bad Kid* Charles Appelstein writes, "For youngsters lacking internal controls fair limits provide an atmosphere of safety and caring, which emphasizes adult-child relationships as well as social functioning" (Applestein, 1998, p. 175). If your program's treatment efforts do not effectively intervene, your clients may experience adulthoods filled with broken relationships, inability to hold on to steady employment, and possibly trouble with the law. As you can see from the examples you have read in this chapter, children who do not know the difference between appropriate and inappropriate behavior and who do not know how to employ appropriate behavior will experience a great deal of difficulty, conflict, sadness, and disappointment in the residential setting and school. Your steady, consistent interactions with them in the milieu setting limits for their behaviors will gradually teach them to modify their behavior.

RULES AND CONSEQUENCES

Your facility has a set of rules and consequences that are explained to you during your initial job training. The list may seem extensive and cumbersome, especially if you are working with teens whose behavior is more sophisticated than that of smaller children. Rest assured your facility's list of rules and consequences is based upon years of experience working with a specific population of clients and has sound social and behavioral science behind it. Some facilities may incorporate a level system with their rules and consequences. A level system is a program for the children that incorporates different behavioral levels. Children must work their way through the levels in order to earn more privileges because the higher levels contain greater freedom and privileges. Rule violations, poor school performance, and taking care of house responsibilities are among the things that can influence moving up or down the levels. The level system has strong theory and practice supporting this approach, particularly in homes that have a high level of structure and supervision. Whether or not your facility uses a level system as a means of showing consequences for inappropriate behavior and reward for appropriate behavior, the central goal is to teach your children how to modify their behavior at the present time and in the future.

When children are admitted to your facility, they likely receive the list of rules and consequences and the staff or an assigned peer will carefully go over it with each child. It is important that children understand the rules and consequences right from the beginning of their stay at your facility. Staff should encourage them to refer to their copy of the rules when they have a question. Children who are older and have been in more than one placement will tell you, if they are being honest, that rules and consequences are very similar from one facility to another. For most children in residential care, your rules will be relatively familiar.

Oftentimes, as part of their maladaptive manipulation, a new client will tell you the rules were very different at a previous placement, that there was a lot more freedom there. A seven-year-old boy named Jared who just recently arrived at a residential facility was going over the rules with childcare worker Elise. He told Elise that at his previous group home he was allowed to leave the facility and go for a walk through the nearby city streets whenever he wanted to. Elise knew very well that no child his age was permitted to walk unsupervised through the city no matter where he was placed. A new client may question a rule that she knows she had to follow at every other placement. For example, almost every new client that comes to Samantha's Group Home for teen girls asks, "Is it okay for us to have a cell phone?" The program manager laughs to himself each time he hears the question, knowing that children in placement are well aware that no residential programs in their county allow children to have cell phones. Once in a while, a new client tells him that cell phones were permitted at her last placement, which is not the case at all.

In both cases, children are testing limits to see if the adults in charge will hold firm to the rules or will bend and be easily manipulated. For a child in residential placement, testing limits is part of her maneuvers to become familiar with her new environment and ascertain what is accepted and what is not (Trieschman, 1969, p. 63). Your clients instinctively test limits as most children do. Every parent has heard her child say, "Okay, I'll just ask Grandma" or "All my friends' parents let them do it." The manipulative behaviors you will encounter in your clients differ in two major ways from those seen in children who come from functioning homes, however,

1. Children in residential care are significantly more adept at manipulation than the average child is
2. Children in residential care test limits to be sure the limits will hold and ultimately give them the safety and security they so desperately need.

First, your clients are significantly more adept at manipulation than the average child is. Because the only way many of your clients had their basic needs met was through manipulation, these children focused a great deal of attention on perfecting the manipulative behaviors that worked for them. Because in many cases little or no attention or praise was given to them when they exhibited positive behaviors, they did not focus on that area much, but they did put much effort into working the angles with the adults in their world. This is what got them what they wanted and needed most of the time. In fact, a child-care worker who has more than fourteen years' experience always tells new staff when she trains them, "Our kids have PhDs in manipulation."

Second, because your clients have experienced little safety and security in their young lives, they test limits to be sure the limits will hold and ultimately give them the safety and security they so desperately need. As Charles Appelstein writesm "When you treat troubled children with compassion and understanding yet hold them accountable for their actions, the message you send is: 'You are in control of your behavior and you like anyone else will be held responsible for inappropriate conduct.' This is a message of normalcy" (1998, p. 54). Ironically, as they are working hard to find cracks in the structure to get what they think they want, on some level children really do need and want the structure to hold.

Your system of rules and consequences is a key part of that structure. When children ask to have a cell phone at their new placement, knowing that the answer will not be affirmative, they are really testing to see how firmly the structure will hold and if the rules they have been given are really followed. If their test shows them that the rules will be followed, most children will begin to relax and feel that the new environment will be safe for them.

On the other hand, if a child finds out that one or more childcare workers are not following the rules and consequences while they are on shift, the message is that structure and safety will not surround them in the facility, and, as a result, the child may not be safe there. Ask anyone who has worked in the field for more that a few years: if only one childcare worker disregards at least some of the rules shift after shift, the result will be one or more out-of-control children. Why does this happen? It is because children quickly recognize that the structure has been disrupted and soon begin to feel unsafe and start acting out. They will remember the dysfunctional environments from which they came and will begin to revert to at least some of the behaviors that worked for them there. Even youngsters who have been doing particularly well in the program can be nudged toward acting out behaviors by a childcare worker who thinks that he or she does not need to follow all the rules. The children in your care want you and your coworkers to assist them by placing limits on their behavior (Appelstein, 1998).

Let us look at an example. An overnight staff member began to allow children to get up after lights out and watch television once the evening staff had left for the day. The rules at the facility clearly stated that children were not to be out of their rooms after lights out, with a few exceptions, such as to use the restroom. Even if granted permission to be out of their rooms for a specific purpose, they must return to bed as soon as possible. Allowing the children to get up and watch television was an obvious rule violation, so the overnight staff member made all the kids promise not to tell or he would lose his job. All agreed. At first, the children were thrilled. One bragged to his classmates at school that he had seen Jay Leno for the first time in his whole life, but the euphoria did not last long. Soon, one of the children began to act out after returning from school. His psychologist tried unsuccessfully to get to the root of the boy's decompensation. One evening the child became escalated and threw a chair across the room. Childcare workers intervened and as the boy calmed down he began to cry. Eventually, he told the childcare workers about what the overnight worker was doing. When the supervisor was informed the overnight worker's employment was terminated. With a new overnight staff member who followed the rules, the boy's behavior stabilized.

When childcare workers do not follow one or more rules, they inevitably have to ask the children to lie to cover up their failure to do their jobs appropriately. In essence, the children become accomplices in the "crime." As you know, this is clearly a boundary problem, but it also puts pressure on children who are placed at the facility for serious treatment issues. Inevitably, they will intuit that what the childcare workers are doing is wrong. In addition they will be conflicted when reconciling the benefits of the rule laxity to them, for example, getting to stay up late, with the feeling of uncertainty over whether they can trust that any of the structure will hold in the future. Although it might be fun at first to stay up late, reality soon sets in that childcare workers cannot be trusted to follow their own rules. Many children will recall the dysfunctional environments from which they were removed and begin to revert to their old maladaptive behaviors.

CONSEQUENCES FOR RULE VIOLATIONS

Although the rules are in place to enforce program structure and set limits for behavior, they are also designed to teach your clients about inappropriate behavior and provide natural consequences for that type of behavior. As we have discussed, this is imperative because so many of your clients were never taught what constitutes acceptable and unacceptable behavior, and many adapted negative behavior patterns as they survived extreme dysfunction. Rules and consequences play a key role in stopping a cycle that may result in a serious personality disorder. In addition, giving natural consequences for inappropriate behavior lets your clients know "that staff cares enough to 'deal with their behavior" and that "the staff member can maintain structure in the milieu keeping the residents safe no matter what" (Harris, 2003, p. 11).

Consequences for inappropriate behavior tackle the common problem of negative attention seeking because now there is no reward given for the negative behavior. Instead, a negative in the form of a consequence is the result of the inappropriate behavior. In this way, children learn that inappropriate behavior has consequences now and in the future. Youngsters will have to replace negative attention-seeking behaviors because they no longer bring about the desired effect. As a childcare worker you help to teach this important behavior and assist the children in your care in making this important behavior modification that will remain with them for the rest of their lives and result in a more productive future. Children who received negative attention through throwing temper tantrums while living in their family home will soon realize that the attention they now get is not what they desire. When they begin to lose privileges or drop a level on a level system, they will slowly recognize that the negative attention-seeking behavior is no longer working for them. They will begin to work toward changing that behavior with the help of childcare workers in their residential facility.

In addition, children will learn to replace inappropriate behaviors they have learned with more positive ones as they begin to recognize that there are consequences for those behaviors. For example, many of the children in residential treatment grew up hearing all of the adults around them using profane language. The adults used it when they talked to each other, and parents likely used bad language when talking to their children, especially when they were angry. Worst of all, parents may have called their children vulgar names even when the children were very young. Consequently, swearing is a frequent rule violation in most facilities, especially for children who are new to placements. Children who grew up where swearing was accepted will use a curse word just like any other word with no conception that the word is offensive to others. Rules and consequences prohibiting cursing work to teach children that swearing is not acceptable and consequences will result. For older children, staff may extrapolate to a future job situation where bad language may result in termination. For most children, the light bulb goes on very quickly. They will begin to catch themselves before the word exits their lips, and after time even the worst offenders will stop swearing, with only a few slips when they are angry or upset. In residential treatment, such "limit setting experiences are crucial to the child. They involve the child's development of a healthy sense of inhibition in which the child learns that what he or she wanted to do is not safe or socially appropriate" (Siegel & Hartzell, 2003, p. 189).

THE PROMPT, WARNING, CONSEQUENCE METHOD

It is imperative that rules are enforced fairly and evenly. Children, always on the look out for favoritism, will detect with radar precision when a staff member is bending rules and procedures for the benefit of a particular client. You will need to establish a consistent procedure to follow when giving out consequences and stick to it without allowing personal feelings and prejudices to enter into the equation.

Here is a solid modus operandi called the prompt, warning, consequence (PWC) method that you can practice when giving consequences for rule violations:

1. Give a prompt (P), indicating that you are aware of the rule violation and need for the behavior to stop.
2. If the behavior continues, give a warning (W), letting the child know exactly what will happen if the behavior continues.
3. If the behavior does not stop following the prompt and warning, let the client know immediately that you have no choice but to give a consequences (C).

When children violate a rule, first give them a prompt. You have put them on notice that a rule has been violated and consequences may follow if they do not stop or change the behavior. Second, if the behavior does not stop or change, let them know that you are giving them fair warning that if the behavior does not end they will receive a consequence. State clearly and precisely exactly what that consequence will be. If you need to refer to your facility's list of consequences, do not hesitate to do so before giving the warning. Finally, if the behavior still continues, immediately tell them that you have to give them the consequences that you had previously stated. Restate exactly what the consequence is when you tell them.

When using the PWC method, refer to the rules and consequences as a separate entity, a binding third party that dictates what you must do as part of your job. In this way, giving consequences is not personal but rather a requirement as mandated by the rules of the facility. As you give consequences, you may even express remorse for having to do so or verbally express the wish that the client had made a different choice. By emphasizing the aspect of choice in the situation you allow children to correct their behavior and in doing so you support children to make good choices and control their own behavior. You will notice that the PWC method allows children to make a choice at several different points. As Appelstein points out, "When a troubled child begins to act out, warnings and other supportive interventions are used to encourage him to control his behavior. The objective is to support his capacity to make good decisions on his own" (Appelstein, 1998, p. 176). The PWC approach not only allows the child to learn the difference between right and wrong behavior, but it also teaches children to utilize, build, and strengthen their own internal controls through the choice they are given.

Let us look at an example of how PWC might play out in a residential setting. Childcare worker Gina heard her client Sara cursing as she talked to her peers. "Sara, please don't use that language." Gina told Sara, "My ears are burning!" Gina covered her ears as if to protect them. (Using humor will often diffuse a situation and completely change the tone of an interaction with a client.) Unfortunately, Sara did not listen and continued swearing intermittently. Gina addressed her again, "Sara, I need for you to stop using bad words, or I will have to give you a twenty-four-hour loss of your telephone privilege, which I really don't want to do." This time Sara did not use a curse word for a few minutes, but she soon resumed the behavior. Gina walked over to Sara and said, "I'm sorry, but you have violated a rule after I gave you fair warning. I don't have any choice but to give you twenty-four-hour loss of your telephone privileges." Sara briefly tried to argue her case. Gina continued, "I really wish you had made a different choice so I wouldn't have to do this."

In the preceding example, the situation was handled appropriately. First, a prompt was given to let the client know that the behavior needed to stop and to allow her to make a choice to stop or continue. A warning came next, letting the client know that a consequence was imminent and again giving her the choice to stop or continue. When the warning was not heeded, the childcare worker followed through with appropriate consequences. Next, Gina clearly stated what consequence she had given right then and there. Gina referred to the rules as a separate entity that dictated what she had to do to fulfill her job. Finally, she expressed remorse and the wish that her client had made a different choice. There was nothing personal involved—just Gina doing her job. If you follow this procedure consistently your clients, although they may never tell you this, will see you as a fair person who does not play favorites and treats everyone equally. You will earn their respect.

When using PWC, follow-through is critical. If you are to be respected as an authority figure, your clients must know you mean what you say and say what you mean (France, 1993). A lack of follow-through can result in your clients not taking you seriously. Children will quickly recognize which childcare workers mean what they say and follow through and which who do not. The childcare worker without follow-through will find that on his or her shift children will be much more likely to push limits than they do on shifts with childcare workers who exhibit consistent and good follow-through.

It is important to tell clients as soon as possible that you have given them a consequence (France, 1993). Children become upset when they find out hours later or even the next morning. When you give out delayed consequences, the teaching effect of the limit set is often likely to be lost because the opportunity to discuss the consequence and process with the client could not occur (Mayer, 1958). Better to be upfront and communicating with the client throughout the interaction. Using the PWC method ensures that you do this because the message is reinforced at the various stages of the procedure.

Always remain calm and composed when using the PWC method. Never allow yourself to become upset or angered by a client's misbehavior. As Harris notes, "If a staff member becomes angered, reacting in a loud, threatening tone when a child breaks a rule, it might enable the youngster to hold onto the belief that all adults are abusive" (Harris, 2003, p. 11). If you find that a client is "getting to you," it is time to ask a coworker to step in and handle the situation. Discussing this issue with your supervisor would be a good idea because she or he can offer some insight into your problems with maintaining a professionally calm demeanor.

If a child is engaging in out-of-control or dangerous behavior, the previous procedure should not be used. If a child is out of control, de-escalation techniques should be employed. First, uninvolved clients should be placed in a separate area for a crisis time out to keep them safe while the staff works with the out-of-control client. Most facilities train the staff in methods of crisis intervention like Pro-Act or Crisis Prevention Institute (CPI). When working with an out-of-control client, you must employ the principles of the crisis intervention program your facility uses. Because most facilities are required to train staff in a crisis intervention method that may include behavioral restraints, we will not go into the principles of crisis intervention here.

If a child is engaging in dangerous behavior that violates a house rule, you must make firm, yet calm, demands for the behavior to stop. Use short sentences. If demands do not work, do not be averse to begging, which often works in these types of situations. For example, a child has a pair of safety scissors and is threatening to cut on herself. Staff should firmly say, "Janice, please give me the scissors." This statement may be repeated three or four times waiting after each for the client to choose to comply. When Janice does not comply, staff should switch tactics saying, "Janice, please give me the scissors. I really don't want to see you hurt yourself. Please give them to me now." Stay with the client until she complies.

USING "I" STATEMENTS

The use of "I" statements is very helpful in situations from simple interactions to crisis situations in which consequences may have to be given. Using I statements involves taking the word you out of your verbal responses during the situation as much as possible. The focus should be what you the childcare worker need the client to do, your feelings about the situation, and what response you will have to make. Here are some examples of you statements and how they can be re-framed as I statement:

> You: Stop swearing.
> I: I need to have you stop swearing.

> You: You can't watch television. Turn it off right now.
> I: I'm sorry but your television privilege has been removed. I'm going to have to ask you to turn it off.

> You: You're being very obnoxious. Stop it.
> I: I'm very disappointed by your behavior this afternoon. Can we talk about some ways we can help you do better?

Notice that the you statements take an accusatory or blaming tone while the I statements are more conciliatory, and less judgmental and authoritarian. Children will respond more favorably to I statements because they feel that the childcare worker is willing to help them and work with them rather than scolding them. This works especially well with children who have a problem with authority because it removes the authoritarian nature of the request. Request is the key concept here. As a childcare worker, using I statements combined with the PWC method means that you are not telling but you are asking. Asking gives the child a choice. Telling implies and authority figure looming over them. Using these tools shows that you respect them, and in turn they will begin to respect you.

POWER STRUGGLES

Power struggles are something to avoid whenever dealing with rule violations or giving consequences. A power struggle occurs when you go head to head with a child, demanding compliance while the child continually refuses. The dynamic of a power struggle occurs when "both parties get themselves into a position where to capitulate would mean to lose face" (Trieschman, 1969, p. 92).

Here are some reasons why power struggles are a bad idea:

1. Your clients may have developed power struggles as a maladaptive means of getting what they want from adults. They may thrive on the negative attention, knowing from experience the end result will be a capitulating adult.
2. Children with oppositional defiant disorder, which often occurs in teens in residential treatment, will instinctively rebel against the authoritarian stance a power struggle will elicit from you.
3. A power struggle is likely to cause the child's behavior to become escalated.
4. When you are involved in a power struggle with a client, you are unlikely to win.

A power struggle for your clients is most likely one of the maladaptive behaviors they developed to survive in their difficult home situations. Anyone who is a parent knows that children frequently get into power struggles with their mothers and fathers. Imagine if your child was not redirected from the power struggle and learned that the power struggle worked and got him what he wanted. Add in a chaotic and dysfunctional living situation and you are describing the behavior of the children in care. They naturally attempt to get into power struggles with adults, but they have learned the behavior well and are much better at it than the average child. If you get into a power struggle with them you are simply reinforcing the maladaptive behavior. You are saying to your clients—in effect—this works, this gets you attention, this engages authority figures. Engaging in a power struggle with them simply perpetuates the behavior.

As you know, many of the children with whom you work are diagnosed with oppositional defiant disorder. Because of this, they do not trust authority figures. Your activity as a childcare worker attempts to show them that there are positive authority figures who will take care of them, set limits for their behavior, and be consistent and fair. A power struggle is contradictory with this message. The back and forth can escalate on both sides. Voices may be raised. Soon you are beginning to appear like the authority figure in their pasts who did not treat them in an appropriate manner. In effect, if you allow it, the child can turn you into exactly what she believes authority figures to be—angry, loud, demanding and ready to verbally fight with a child. Avoiding the power struggle allows you to keep your demeanor calm and your approach to the situation fair. In this way you model the positive authority figure—exactly what the child needs.

Because a primary goal of your work is to keep your clients as calm and even in mood as possible, a power struggle becomes counterproductive. If you get into a power struggle with a child, his behavior is likely to escalate as the power struggle inevitably does the same. Many children in care have anger management issues. They are angry about their situation, and angry that the adults in their lives have let them down, angry that they cannot live at home with them parents. As it escalates, a power struggle can tap into that well of anger, and the child may unleash a reaction that is out of proportion to the precipitating event. Getting into a power struggle with one of your clients will actually create a situation of escalation that you naturally try to avoid as you provide a consistent, nurturing environment for the children in your care.

When you engage in a power struggle with a child, you are most unlikely to emerge the winner. Because your clients have learned and practiced power struggles as maladaptive behaviors, they have gotten very good at managing them. They have learned how to get what they want from adults by using power struggles. Whether their goal is simply to get attention or to gain a special privilege, their skills in the power struggle are superior to yours—plain and simple. A childcare worker who takes part in a power struggle with a child also loses because the child escalates, a serious incident such as property destruction might occur, and other clients will be upset and their time disrupted by the resulting uproar.

Avoid power struggles by using the PWC method described earlier in this chapter. This approach gives the child a choice and does not demand a particular action from the client. Choice empowers the child and does not engage him in a battle of wills. If you carefully lay out the alternatives and allow the child to choose, your outcome will be more favorable, even if you have to give consequences for noncompliance. In dangerous or crisis situations, when a short, firm command does not work, it is better to soften your approach as described in your facility's crisis intervention method. Getting into a power struggle with an already escalated client will only increase the client's escalation and the potential danger of the situation.

Here are two examples of how this works in practice. Clients informed staff that client Kevin had a cell phone, which was against house rules. A staff person believed she saw Kevin with the cell phone, which he quickly hid under his pillow when he saw the staff person. The staff person said to Kevin, "It looks to me like you hid a cell phone. Is that true?"

"No," Kevin responded. "I don't have any cell phone."

"Well, a couple of people said they have seen you with a phone," the staff person told him.

"I don't have a phone," Kevin said his voice beginning to get louder.

"I really need to have you give me the phone because you know it is against the rules," the staff responded.

"Look," Kevin told the staff person, "I already told you I don't have no phone. Now get out of here and leave me alone."

The staff person retreated and reported the incident to her supervisor. The supervisor told her staff that she did the right thing in the situation. Continuing to demand the cell phone would only have escalated the situation and would not likely have resulted in the phone's being turned in. The supervisor went to Kevin and informed him that if he gave her the cell phone before she left for the day he would not receive consequences. Kevin reached under his pillow, pulled out the phone, and handed it to the supervisor. Giving the child a choice rather than going head to head with him resulted in the desired outcome.

In the second example, a pair of scissors that one of Martha's clients checked out was missing. Staff asked the client who checked out the scissors to return them, and the client said the scissors simply disappeared when she went to the bathroom. Martha was concerned because she had some clients in the facility who had histories of cutting on themselves. She asked all the girls where the scissors were, and all denied knowing anything about them. After Martha and another staff did a cursory search of common areas and did not find the scissors, it was time to choose a different strategy. Since the scissors were safety scissors that could not be used as a weapon, the situation did not pose a serious threat; however, staff remained concerned because of the clients with cutting histories. The staff could have searched each girl's room, but they rejected this option because a power struggle and escalation of client behavior was likely to result. Instead, they informed all of the girls that the house would be put on shut down, which meant no outings, computer, or television, until the scissors were returned.

"I am really worried that someone might use them to hurt themselves, so I really need to get them back," Martha told them. (Note the use of I statements.)

The clients were told that a basket would be placed on the dining room table, and the scissors could be returned to that basket—no questions asked. Within a half hour, Martha found the missing scissors in the basket.

LIMIT SETTING DIFFICULTIES

Sometimes staff members have trouble giving consequences to clients. Childcare workers may be only a few years older than are the clients with whom they work and may not be comfortable with their role as an authority figure. They may not have grown into a concept of themselves as the adult in charge. In most cases, training and experience will assist younger childcare workers in becoming more comfortable with their role as an authority figure. Understanding the importance of having strong role models for appropriate adult authority figures and the clients' need for the safety and security of a consistently maintained and structured milieu helps. Knowing that children in residential placement do not need more friends but instead need competent adults to protect them and meet their needs allows childcare workers to see that the authority figure fills a much-needed void for these kids. If a childcare worker is still having difficulty taking on the mantle of an authority figure that sets limits for the children in her care, she or he should talk to the supervisor.

Some childcare workers who are having difficulty with setting limits and the consequences mistakenly believe that children will not like them if they are given consequences. Just the opposite is true because our clients "truly want the adults in their world to exert external controls that can keep them on the right path; without such limits, life as they know it becomes scary and confusing" (Appelstein, 1998, p. 175). In fact, as Trieschman points out, "Most children need external controls, may even ask for them, and will view the worker who never interferes as being frightened and inadequate" (Trieschman, 1969, p. 89). It is quite true that children will respect and, yes, like the staff members who are firm but fair at setting limits. If you are not comfortable with giving consequences or setting limits for your clients' behavior, talk to your supervisor as soon as possible. He or she will be able to help and guide you to improving in this important area of milieu therapy.

As you work with your clients and set limits for their behavior, do not become discouraged if you see behaviors recur after consequences are given. Oftentimes, childcare workers interpret repetition of the same misbehavior as a sign that their approach is not working. You must remember that the maladaptive behaviors displayed by your clients were learned over several years, and as complex learned reactions to difficult living situations, these behaviors are well-engrained into each child's way or relating to his world. Durrant writes,

> No punishment or consequence will ensure that a particular behavior never recurs. The residential placement is a period of trial error, and slip-ups will not be uncommon. The fact that a resident "re-offends" after having been given a consequence for misbehavior does not mean the consequence was not severe enough. It simply means that the process of learning competence and self control takes time. Our consequences . . . must aim primarily to provide an opportunity for young people to discover something about themselves and their control. (Durrant, 1993, p. 112)

Be patient. Keep an eye out for even the smallest successes, and above all do not get discouraged. Remember: "A crucial task of the child care worker is to help the child learn new ways of behaving" (Trieschman, 1969, p. 56). Your work should be aimed in the direction of teaching and knowing that the student will respond and learn when he or she is ready. View repeated misbehaviors as practice toward learning a new coping strategy or way to behave. The childcare worker makes inroads toward modifying a child's behavior by hundreds of tiny interactions that happen over weeks and even months, but rest assured, your efforts in the practice of milieu therapy are making a difference.

CHAPTER 6 REVIEW

1. Most children in foster care grew up in dysfunctional homes where they learned maladaptive behaviors that helped them survive in difficult circumstances. Now that these children have entered treatment, it is time for them to replace the maladaptive behaviors with more positive behaviors that will help them be more successful in their lives.

2. Childcare workers help children learn what behaviors are inappropriate and what they need to change through setting limits for inappropriate behaviors.

3. A facility's set of rules assists the childcare worker in setting limits for behavior. Some programs have a level system that works with structured achievement levels. By performing the requirements of each level, the child can earn additional privileges. Inappropriate behaviors may cause a child to move down one or more levels and lose privileges that have been gained.

4. Children who have been in residential care are very familiar with house rules. House rules are fairly consistent from one facility to another, so children will be acquainted with a new facility's rules.

5. Children will frequently test limits, especially when new to the program or when working with a new staff, to see whether or not the limits are going to hold. All children do this from time to time, but children in residential care are more adept at manipulation than the average child is. Also, children in residential care test limits to make sure that the safety and security limits will actually stay in place.

6. If the rules are not followed by all childcare workers with consistency, children will begin to feel unsafe and may begin to display acting out behaviors.

7. Natural consequences for rule violations are an important part of teaching children that inappropriate behaviors do have consequences, as they will now and in the future. Children will be motivated to learn more positive behaviors when they know that consequences will result from negative behaviors.

8. It is imperative that all childcare workers handle consequences fairly and consistently.

9. One way to ensure that consequences are being enforced fairly is to use the PWC method. When the negative behavior occurs, staff members should give a prompt, indicating that the childcare worker is aware of the behavior and needs the behavior to stop. If the behavior continues, a warning should be given, letting the child know exactly what will happen if the behavior continues. Finally, if the behavior continues, the child should be told immediately that there is no choice but to assign the consequence that was detailed in the warning.

10. The PWC method is effective because every step of the way it gives children a choice, which empowers and allows them to practice self-control.

11. When dealing with a rule violation, it is very helpful for the childcare worker to refer to the rules as a separate entity that controls what the childcare worker must do. In this way, it is not personal; it is simply the childcare worker doing her or his job.

12. Another helpful technique when dealing with escalating be - havior or rule violations is to use I statements. Using I statements takes the accusatory or blaming tone out and replaces it with a more conciliatory, less judgmental, and less authoritarian tone.

13. A power struggle is something a childcare worker wants to avoid whenever possible. Using the PWC method and I statements can be very helpful in this regard. Remember that giv-

ing children a choice is most likely to produce a positive outcome.

14. Some childcare workers have trouble giving consequences and
enforcing rules because they mistakenly believe that children
will not like them if they do. Children in actuality want guidance and limits from adults as much as they might protest. The
absence of limits feels unsafe to children, especially to children
who are emotionally disturbed.

15. Childcare workers should not become discouraged if behaviors reoccur after consequences have been given. Children learn
maladaptive behaviors over a long period of time, so they will
not unlearn them over night.

EXERCISE

Think about a time when you had to set limits for a child at a facility
where you work or have worked in the past. Consider the events carefully. Describe the incident without using the actual names of clients.
Then write three things that you could have done better and write
three ways you might have acted to improve the outcome of the situation, using some of the suggestions offered in this chapter.

Describe the Incident

Things I Could Have Done Better

1.

2.

3.

Ways to Improve the Outcome

1.

2.

3.

Chapter 7

ELEMENTS OF MILIEU THERAPY: REWARDING POSITIVE BEHAVIOR

Most of the children with whom you work were not parented effectively when they were growing up in their dysfunctional family homes. Not only were they not taught that there were consequences for negative behaviors, but also they were not rewarded or praised for positive behaviors. As we have seen, without being praised for accomplishments large or small, they may have developed low self-esteem and may have given up on trying to be "good children" at home and at school. A child who does not receive any reward or praise from her parent for earning a "B" on her report card or winning a good citizen award in first grade may wonder why she tries at all. She may opt for seeking negative attention at home and at school, which to her seems easier to get and more freely given. You have no doubt heard the saying that negative attention is better than no attention at all. Your clients learn this at a very early age.

As children grow and approach adulthood, their negative attention seeking has more and more serious consequences for their future. In school they will continue to be underachievers and mistrustful of authority. They may miss the opportunity to attend college or other post-secondary school education because they develop a dislike of school settings. Later, when they must work to earn a living, negative behavior will have far-reaching consequences resulting in repeated instances of lost employment. At your facility, their negative behavior will create a loss of program levels or a buildup of restrictions of privileges that can leave them feeling discouraged and hopeless.

Teaching children that positive behavior will be rewarded is just as important as teaching them that negative behavior has consequences.

In fact, a primary focus of your work should be rewarding positive behavior—large or small. Your clients need to know that they will be rewarded in life if they behave appropriately. Durrant (1993) notes, "Within the residential program, this means staff looking for any examples—no matter how small and seemingly insignificant of successful, competent, non-problem behavior and drawing attention to them" (p. 88). The children in your care need to know that it feels good to be good and that achievement will pay dividends now and in their future.

Praise and reward for good behavior will help to build a client's self-esteem. You probably have seen the manifestations of low self-esteem in many of your clients. Your efforts to praise and reward them for positive behavior will help to build their self esteem and make them more confident and capable as they move toward adulthood (Appelstein, 1998).

REWARDING POSITIVE BEHAVIOR

Your facility most likely has a system of reward for positive client behavior. Clients on good behavior may earn the highest level and increased privileges, or they may earn more allowance. They may also earn money or increased privileges for good grades or work toward a treatment goal. A good program has many elements worked into the facility's policies and procedures that reward good behavior and achievement. One facility, for example, has a daily chart that staff use to track children's behavior and responsibilities in the milieu on every shift. Based on their performance on the daily chart, the amount the girls receive in allowance is reduced or increased. Some girls make thirty dollars or more each week. In addition, the top two performers on the daily charts for that week are allowed to choose two of the weekend activities. At another facility, a level system is in place. Here the boys have to meet certain criteria to move up each of four levels. Those who have reached the highest levels have increased privileges, including self-passes in the community, increased phone time, and first choice for outings and activities. A facility for teen boys offers the children the opportunity to earn money for progress toward monthly treatment goals. Each month the boys sit down with the program social worker and talk about behavioral challenges they need to work on. A list of four is agreed upon and transferred to a treatment goal form. Staff are briefed on the new treatment goals for each boy every month. The childcare workers then give the boys points for making progress on each goal. At the end of a quarter, the points are totaled up and the boys get to go shopping to spend the money they have earned, or they can elect to put it into their savings account.

Many programs offer clients on restriction a chance to work off earned restriction of privileges by doing chores, writing an essay, or reading an article that applies to the offense. This provides clients the opportunity to instantly turn around their negative behavior while working in a positive way toward a reward. As Appelstein (1998) points out, "When we acknowledge a child's efforts to improve, we support his earliest strivings, affirming for him where he is, not where he should be. In response the child will feel better about himself and be more motivated to take responsibility for his actions" (p. 44). When children has gone through a bad period and racked up consequences as a result, the acknowledging of a desire to change their behavior immediately provides the motivation to do better. These same children might become "buried' by the amount of consequences they have accrued and lack the desire to try to turn around. The reward of working off restriction of privileges gives children a reachable goal—a light at the end of the tunnel—that allows them to get back on track in a relatively short period of time.

For example, Marco was a thirteen-year-old resident at a treatment facility for boys. He had a rough adjustment to the program, and during his first months at his new program he was given several weeks of complete loss of privileges. Being on restriction only seemed to make him angrier and to dislike the program and staff more. He continued to earn more and more consequences for rule violations. Finally, the program social worker at his facility decided to give Marco the opportunity to work off his restriction at a faster rate than that normally allowed by the program. Knowing that Marco was drowning under the weight of his consequences and suspecting that he also had developed a pattern of negative attention seeking, the social worker felt it was important to give him the chance to learn what it felt like to be good and to get out from under the weight of his restriction. At first, Marco did not agree with the new contract and refused to follow through, but he finally latched on to the contract and began to complete the required tasks. The social worker asked staff to freely praise him as he completed his assignments. Soon Marco had finished his contract, and he was off restriction. The transformation was amazing. He was upbeat and proud of his accomplishment. The social worker was pleased to see him feeling so positive. He realized that Marco had, perhaps for the first time, learned that it felt good to be good.

REWARDING WITH PRAISE

Whatever the reward system at your facility, you should utilize it whenever possible to give positive feedback for good behavior. Of course, the simplest way to reward is through praise or verbal feedback, so you should be constantly on the lookout for opportunities to do so. Remember, childcare workers providing milieu therapy are not just disciplinarians doling out consequences; instead childcare workers are also engaging children by rewarding them for positive behavior. In doing so, you will help your clients by

1. Showing them that good behavior is rewarded
2. Helping to transform maladaptive behaviors
3. Building their self-esteem

It is so important to praise your clients and show them that their good behavior is recognized. Not only is appropriate behavior recognized, but also it is rewarded with special praise. To you, it may seem like a small thing to hear "You did a really good job cleaning the kitchen counter," but to a child who has been deprived of praise and looks to you as an authority figure, your words could be worth their weight in gold. Praise is easy to give and is always received with pleasure by your clients even if they do not outwardly show it. When you praise a client it is a good chance to teach manners, too. Praise should always be followed with a simple thank you. It is okay to remind your clients to respond with gratitude for the compliment. One childcare worker has found saying "you're welcome" automatically reminds children that they have missed giving the appropriate response.

Your praise can also help youngsters learn to change their maladaptive behaviors. Praising clients actually directs them toward the correct behavior and away from the incorrect behaviors they may have learned prior to coming to your facility. Regular praise for the modified behavior will result in fewer instances of the maladaptive behavior. At one residential facility, a boy named Troy had difficulty getting along with his peers. He became upset and angry at the slightest provocation and sometimes with no provocation. Especially difficult for him was sharing anything. At a staff meeting, the program manager had emphasized that this behavior needed to be targeted by staff and suggested some way to accomplish this. One of the major approaches was to praise Troy when he displayed appropriate behavior. The childcare workers set out to tackle the task of modifying Troy's negative behavior. At first their praise seemed to have little impact; in fact, it was hard to find anything to praise because Troy constantly screamed and yelled whenever another child used a house toy that Troy thought belonged to him and him alone, even if he was not playing with it at the time. Still, the childcare workers were able to find little things to praise. Things such as "Wow, great sneakers," "Nice job rinsing out your cereal bowl!" and "Thanks for taking the time to open the cabinet door for me. That was so thoughtful" began to chip away at Troy's irritable shell.

One day a childcare worker was supervising the children as they were playing. Troy was building a castle with a large pile of blocks when another child came along with a dump truck and took two of the blocks and put them into the truck bed. The childcare worker saw Troy stop, and his face began to turn red, a sure sign that a tantrum was coming. Troy looked up at the childcare worker, however, took a deep breath, and continued playing. Tantrum averted for the first time. The childcare worker went over to Troy and lavished him with praise for his good choices. Troy beamed and proudly told the childcare worker that he was a good boy. The childcare worker agreed.

When childcare workers praise children, it naturally helps build their self-esteem. Even if you have worked in residential care for only a short time, you know that the children often suffer from low self-esteem, having very little feeling of self-worth or worthiness. Praise goes a long way to help children feel better about themselves. When a caring adult authority figure recognizes that they have done a good job, a child with low self-esteem will simple gobble up that praise. As your team of milieu therapists praise, these children day after day, you will see them begin to blossom and feel better about who they are. Of course, they will still have other issues and need to work on them in the milieu and in therapy that hinder the growth of their self-esteem, but your praise is an essential boost that is needed so much for these children. Praise, too, can recognize small things—a pretty way a girl has done her hair, a nice job coloring a page from a coloring book, an outstandingly well-made bed—the list is endless. Make praise an essential part of your daily work with the children in your care and watch their self-esteem grow.

Kristie was an eight-year-old resident at a group home. Her mother had abandoned her and disappeared, and Kristie had no involvement from other family. She was truly an orphan. (Most children in residential care do have some family or parental involvement throughout their lives.) She was a quiet girl who preferred to remain in the background, rarely interacting with peers or childcare workers. A childcare worker named Anna asked Kristie why she did not ever want to join the group while they were playing. Kristie admitted it was because she was afraid the other children and staff would not like her. In Kristie's mind it was better to stay away than to risk the all-too-familiar rejection she had experienced in her young life. Anna and other childcare workers decided to help Kristie by boosting her self-esteem with praise. They took every opportunity they could find to encourage and praise her. Within a couple of months Kristie began to interact with group play and began to enjoying talking and working with the childcare workers on shift. For Anna the biggest reward was seeing Kristie smile and laugh more and more. To Anna, that was the true test that Kristie was feeling much better about herself.

Also important to keep in mind—clients who are doing well need praise too. Sometimes staff have a tendency to somewhat overlook the good behavior of children who are doing well as they struggle to address the issues of children who are having a hard time. This is only natural. You want to go where you are needed most, but you must try to treat all clients equally whenever possible. Of course, if a client is having a crisis intervention, your attention must be focused on deescalating him, but once the crisis has passed, you should return your focus to all of your clients.

Remember even the clients who are model residents have issues they are working on or they would not be at your facility. Depression and anxiety are common, and even for the over achiever, low self-esteem is likely present. Don't forget to praise their efforts as well. If Kelly, who gets high marks in school, is especially polite and helpful to a peer who is struggling with her math homework, you should praise her for being a positive peer. Let her know how much you appreciate and even admire what she did. On her behavioral charting she should receive high notations.

The bottom line is that you cannot be too generous when it comes to praising your clients as long as your praise is genuine. Children, especially teenagers, spot phony praise with amazing accuracy. But if you are regularly handing out real praise, you will quickly find that children absorb it like sponges and reward you with a smile, even if they do not let you see it.

WORKING WITH BASELINE BEHAVIOR

It is important to establish a baseline for each client's behavior when assigning reward. In simple terms, a child's baseline is behavior that is average or typical for a particular client. Baselines provide a yardstick that allows you to observe behaviors that reach beyond the normal and indicate progress or effort that is rewardable or praiseworthy. On the other side, behavior that is below baseline may indicate the need for additional counseling and assistance, thus providing early warning of potential difficulty for a client. Most facilities have treatment teams in place that will determine each client's baseline behavior. If baselines have not already been discussed with you, ask your supervisor about each of your client's baselines so that you will be better prepared on shift.

Without a consideration of baselines, some clients would never receive high marks or praise for their behaviors and responsibilities in the facility. The child who struggles with keeping her room clean would never get high marks in that area, whereas the child who has little problem with keeping her room clean would always get the highest notations. A child who struggles with overcoming a swearing habit would never get high praise for his communication, but the children who communicate more effectively would see the opposite. How then could we encourage the child who struggles and needs improvement?

Baselines are the answer. If a child who has a bad swearing problem goes a whole shift without swearing, he should earn praise. Having a low baseline in the area of language, a shift without swearing would be a definite improvement for him. Baselines are a measure of the true level of achievement children have in any area. When children move above that level, they should be rewarded.

Let us look at an example of baselines at work. Thirteen-year-old Kelly has no problems with her personal hygiene. She showers regularly and washes her hair, which is usually styled neatly in a ponytail. She brushes her teeth and flosses two times a day. Her clothes are always neat and stylish. By comparison hygiene is a problem for thirteen-year-old Marcy. She hates to shower and does not always brush her teeth each day. Sometimes she sleeps in her clothes and tries to wear those same clothes the next day. As you can see, in the area of hygiene, Kelly's baseline is much higher than is Marcy's. It would be unrealistic to expect that Marcy could achieve Kelly's level overnight, and it would be unfair to compare Marcy to Kelly. Each of your clients comes to you with unique sets of strengths and weaknesses.

Keeping Marcy's baseline in mind, you would want to look for improvements, however small, in what she does normally. If you notice Marcy in the bathroom before bed brushing her teeth, you are witnessing a praiseworthy accomplishment. You might tell her what a good job she has done, give her a high five, and write positive marks for the evening in the area of hygiene. If one afternoon Marcy appears with clean, nicely combed hair, she should be praised for her effort. As time goes on, you will likely see that the consistent praise will result in some positive changes in Marcy's hygiene. She may never have the grooming habits of Kelly, but because all children naturally enjoy praise and positive feedback, Marcy will seek that praise and make changes in her hygiene. If Kelly, on the other hand, is looking especially well-groomed one day, that is worthy of praise as well.

CHALLENGES TO REWARDING POSITIVE BEHAVIOR

Sometimes it takes effort to find things to praise in some of your clients, especially those who are depressed or going through hard times or whose maladaptive behaviors are especially difficult and troublesome. *It is important to know that these are the children who need positive feedback and reward the most!* The challenge for you is to find as many instances to praise as possible. Even if you simply say, "I love that top you're wearing!" or "Good game of basketball. Your jump shot is really improving," you are helping to turn the tide that will lead to your client's seeking the positive more and more. It is also very important that you "reward them when they improve their behavior. Sometimes this means praising a child whose actions fall short of our expectations. A second grader who was sent out of the classroom ten times last week, for example, should be complimented for being sent out only seven times this week" (Appelstein, 1998, p. 44). If you have a difficult time finding ways to praise a particular client, realize that this child very much needs your praise and reward. Look hard for small triumphs and successes. Ask your supervisor for suggestions that will assist in your efforts to praise the difficult to praise.

Gary was a resident at a group home where he was a constant behavioral problem. He delighted in whatever negative attention he could get from childcare workers and his peers. He even embarrassed staff and peers with his disruptive behavior on outings. Once when the children had gone to see a movie, he continued to talk loudly after the movie had started, and after other patrons complained, the whole group was asked to leave the theater. Gary was not exactly a hit with his peers. Staff, too, had a hard time having good feelings about him, and many tried to avoid him altogether. Gary, on the other hand, was completely undeterred and seemed to thrive on the negative responses he got as a result of his behavior. He had dropped to the lowest level and received other consequences, but this did not seem to have any effect. Discouraged, a group of childcare workers sat down with their program's social worker to discuss "the Gary problem."

Among the suggestions the social worker offered was to consider Gary's baseline behavior and reward him whenever he went above his baseline. Almost immediately after the childcare workers began to take into account Gary's baseline and praise him for rising above it, they started to see a change in him. Gary received the first instances of praise with a look of surprise, as though he had never experienced encouragement. Then he began to ask why he was being praised, as though he did not trust that the childcare workers were being genuine. After a few months, he was still disruptive, but that behavior was improving and so were his relationships with peers and staff. One child-care worker told the social worker, "I can't believe I'm saying this, but I actually like that kid!" Were it not for a consideration of Gary's base-line behavior, none of this would have occurred.

As with giving consequences for negative behavior, praise and be-havioral rewards do not change a child overnight. Quite the opposite is true: "positive interactions are vitally important, but they need to occur over and over again. There are no quick fixes for children who have experienced inadequate care in their first five years of life" (Ap-pelstein, 1998, p. 41). Improvements to a child's self-esteem, mood and behavior are affected by praise, and behavioral rewards happen gradually over time. For a relatively small number of children it may take a very long time to effect change. It may not be until a client leaves your facility and perhaps goes through another year or more of treatment and behavioral reinforcement that he will begin to manifest change in his self-esteem, mood, and behavior. In any case, this does not mean that your efforts are not useful or that they are not helping the child. Your work with this client is just part of the greater whole of his treatment that will hopefully in the future begin—as a whole—to have an effect on his behavior.

THE BENEFITS OF REWARDING YOUR CLIENTS

As you reward your clients you will see many of them begin to en-joy the praise and seek it when they are able. You likely will see more modification of client behavior through rewards than you do through punishment. It is just human nature, and children respond especially to praise and reward. In fact, you should make an effort to praise each client at least two times per shift. This can be a challenge, especially when a child is acting out or out of control, but the two times per shift is a good goal to have in your mind. It helps you focus as much, if not more, on reward rather than on consequence, which is the appropri-ate focus to maintain. You are doing your job well if your focus is more on praise than on consequence. Yes, sometimes you must give conse-quences, but you can always freely give genuine praise.

Many childcare workers are surprised to find that when children are rewarded and praised, they are more likely to behave in kind to others. Indeed, as you model that appropriate behavior includes recognizing the achievement and accomplishments of others, children will begin to incorporate that behavior into their own. Do not be surprised if a client compliments you on the nice jacket you are wearing or tells you that you did a good job making the sandwiches for the beach outing. It means that they are paying attention and your influence on them is effecting positive change.

CHAPTER 7 REVIEW

1. The children in your care were not parented effectively when they were growing up in dysfunctional homes, and as a result, they were not rewarded for positive behavior in addition to not being consistently given consequences for inappropriate behavior. The lack of reward for positive behavior causes many children to give up on trying to do well. In fact, many seek negative attention because it is more readily given.

2. Teaching children that positive behavior is rewarding is equally as important as teaching them that negative behavior has consequences. Children need to know that it feels good to be good and that achievement will pay a dividend now and in their future.

3. Praise and reward for good behavior will also help to build your clients' self-esteem and help transform maladaptive behaviors.

4. Childcare workers should use their facility's system of rewarding positive behavior regularly and fairly. Varying from facility to facility a reward system may include earning points to move up a level, receiving more money on their allowance, or earning points on daily behavioral charts.

5. Many programs give children the opportunity to work off accumulated earned restriction of privileges. This practice works well because children often feel buried by restriction, and the chance to clear their restriction results in an immediate need to

turn around their behavior while seeing their restriction disappear.

6. One of the most important ways to reward children in care is to praise them. Reward through positive verbal feedback is direct and simple, but its impact is strong and significant.

7. Verbal praise shows children that their good behavior will be recognized and rewarded.

8. Childcare workers need to keep in mind each child's baseline behaviors when assigning rewards. The baseline is what is normal for that child. Whereas one child may have a baseline of keeping her room in good order, another child may struggle with her room clean. The first child's baseline is much higher than the second's. It would not be reasonable to expect the second child to come up to the level of the first. Having a lower baseline for a small improvement, such as making her bed that day, deserves praise.

9. Childcare workers should bear in mind that the child they find difficult to praise is probably the one who needs their praise the most.

10. Although praise and reward do not change a child overnight, over time the positive approach does make a difference in the life of a troubled child.

11. Childcare workers will likely see more modification of behavior through rewards that they do through consequences.

12. Make an effort to praise each child a minimum of two times per shift.

EXERCISES

Exercise One

On the spaces below, make a list of ten ways you can praise a difficult-to-praise child. You may have a particular child in mind when you make the list, or you can simply choose to make a generalized list that would apply to a variety of children.

1. _____

2. _____

3. _____

4. _____

5. _____

6. _____

7. _____

8. _____

9. _____

10. _____

Exercise Two

Write down five elements of the program at your facility that are designed to reward the children in your care. Then describe how you have used each element and how effective each is in your view. Remember not to use names of specific clients when completing this exercise.

1. Program Element:

   Use Evaluation:

2. Program Element:

   Use Evaluation:

3. Program Element:

   Use Evaluation:

4. Program Element:

   Use Evaluation:

5. Program Element:

   Use Evaluation:

Chapter 8

ELEMENTS OF MILIEU THERAPY: ROLE MODELING

Sandy's mother Joan suffered from bipolar disorder. It was difficult for her to get through most days because she dealt with crushing bouts of depression. When she was depressed, Joan often could not get off the couch in the living room of the one-bedroom apartment she shared with her daughter. On those days, ten-year-old Sandy would have to find food for herself one way or another. Joan had taught her daughter how to beg for money on the streets. Sandy knew to tell the people she approached that she was lost and needed money to use the pay phone to call her mother to come and get her. Joan made her daughter practice this story over and over until she got it perfect. By the end of a day of begging, Sandy had often raised ten dollars to buy food for herself and her mother.

When Joan was depressed, she did not bathe or brush her hair or teeth—sometimes for weeks. She did not do laundry or wash dishes. If Sandy wanted to go to school, sometimes Joan would try to talk her out of it because she did not want to be alone. In order to survive, Sandy quickly learned that she would have to take care of herself and pick up the slack when her mother was having a bad day. She learned how to clean the house, do the laundry and dishes, cook her dinner, and get ready for school on her own.

Sometimes Joan had a manic phase, and during these times she went to bars and stayed out all night, leaving Sandy home alone. Unable to calm down enough to sleep, Joan often brought the party back to her house, and many drunken strangers were there until all hours while Sandy tried to sleep in the bedroom. Joan sometimes would wake up her daughter and tell her to come and join the party.

Sandy knew that when her mother was taking the medication that the doctor prescribed she felt much better. She did not get depressed and was able to take care of herself. Unfortunately, Joan did not like taking her medication. Sandy begged her mother to keep taking her medication, most times to no avail.

Michael never knew his father, and his mother was addicted to heroin. When his mother was unable to care for him as an infant, his aunt took him to live with her. That did not last long because his aunt had her own drug problem. After that he went to live with another aunt, who kept him for a couple of months but could not continue to provide a home for him because she was on welfare and had her own children to consider first. Finally, when he was two he went to live with his grandmother, a bitter woman in her fifties who had difficulty showing love or caring. She neglected Michael as she had her own children. After four years living with his grandmother, child protective services was called and Michael was put into foster care.

One thing most of your clients have in common is that they had few or no positive role models in their lives. Raised in homes destroyed by drugs or alcohol or mental illness that may have stretched over more than one generation, they lived with adults who failed them over and over again (Laursen, 2004). As young children, they did not learn appropriate behavior from the example set by their parents or caregivers. On the contrary, they learned just the opposite. Because your clients did not learn appropriate adult behavior, they risk not knowing how to behave as adults later in their lives. In addition, many of your clients have internalized the negative behaviors they saw in their dysfunctional caregivers, and as a result they frequently exhibit poor behavior.

When five-year-old Robert arrived at his new group home, he constantly used very bad language, especially when he was angry. He often strung expletives together in ways that shocked the staff at his facility. Hearing those words come out of such a young child was hard to fathom. Many childcare workers were very upset by Robert's language. Their supervisor called a meeting and explained a bit of Robert's history to the childcare workers. Raised in a home where his parents operated a drug and prostitution ring, Robert was surrounded by adults who used very bad language constantly. His parents made no attempt to control the swearing of the people they allowed around their children; in fact, they themselves did not refrain from cursing around the children. Further, they frequently directed swear word-filled diatribes at Robert, who was the oldest of six children. As the supervisor explained, it was only natural that Robert followed the lead of the role models in his life. "Now," he said, "we are the new role models, and we must teach him appropriate ways of expressing himself." The childcare workers understood and were less shocked by Robert's words. They began to work hard to model appropriate communication, give him a consequence for swearing, and reward him for using good communication.

In essence, a large part of your work is modeling appropriate behavior for your clients, and role modeling may be "the first and foremost duty of any direct care worker" (Harris, 2003, p. 23). As you interact with your clients, you show them through your behavior, speech, and appearance appropriate self-expression, self-care and behavior. As Roderick Durkin (1990) notes, "Child care workers are themselves influential in providing a more positive prototype for future relationships, particularly in comparison to parents in dysfunctional and often destructive families" (p. 108). You may have noticed that your clients are very watchful of you while you are on shift. They take note of how you carry yourself and your behavior and learn from what they observe.

Positive role modeling encompasses much of your time on shift and is part of every interaction you have with each of your clients. In fact, your work with your clients "should provide numerous opportunities for modeling the kinds of behaviors we would like the children to adopt" (Whittaker, 1979, pp. 85–86). Let us look at a few areas where role modeling is especially important: appearance, demeanor, speech, and authority.

APPEARANCE

As a childcare worker, you have a duty to model appropriate appearance and grooming standards for your clients. Your presentation of yourself should always be professional, neat, and polished. You should be clean and well-groomed, with your hair neat and styled and nails clean and groomed, wear appropriate makeup (do not overdo), and have clean teeth and fresh breath. Deodorant and/or cologne must be used if you have a problem with body odor, especially after exercise, because you will frequently be engaging in physical activities with your clients, such as trips to a local gym or YMCA, walks, softball games, or soccer games. You may want to carry some cologne and/or deodorant or a fresh change of clothes with you if you have an odor problem after exercise. Also, if you are a smoker, you will want to use some kind of fragrance to mask the cigarette smell. (You certainly do not want to be modeling through an obvious odor of cigarettes that it is okay to smoke!) As you well know, children can be brutally honest and will comment if there is the slightest offending scent. The best way to avoid embarrassment is to be prepared in advance.

Your clothing should be chosen carefully, keeping in mind what kinds of activities are planned for your shift that day. In general, a casual outfit is the best bet; however, casual does not mean sloppy or unkempt. Your casual attire should be neat, clean, wrinkle free, and well-matched. Sometimes more formal attire is called for, for example when a play or an opera performance is scheduled. Women may want to wear a dress or pantsuit, and men may want to wear a suit or dress pants and shirt; either way, you will be setting a good model of suitable attire for a variety of settings. You will find that many of the children in your care have never been taught appropriate attire for more formal settings like a church service or even a job interview. As they watch what you wear every day, they will learn what is appropriate and when.

Many facilities, especially those that do behavioral restraints, have strict requirements on footwear. Some will stipulate that childcare workers wear only closed-toed shoes with low or no heels because other shoes may make maintaining balance and position difficult or could result in injury to your feet or ankles when performing a behavioral restraint. It is a good idea in general to wear comfortable shoes to work, such as tennis or athletic shoes. In warmer weather, sandals can be worn if open-toed shoes are permitted, but be sure that you can walk easily in them and can maintain good balance. Heeled shoes or sandals are not recommended because they are not comfortable to walk in and are not good for maintaining balance in an emergency situation.

In general, you should follow the clothing rules your clients must follow at minimum. You should never wear:

1. Tops that are revealing and/or show too much cleavage
2. Blouses or shirts that expose the midriff area
3. Skirts or shorts that are too short (Use the fingertip test: if you let your arm hang straight down and the hem of the garment is above your fingertip, it is too short.)
4. Pants that are too low waisted or that hang below your hip bone;
5. Any clothing that allows any undergarment to show, including bra straps or underpants
6. Any garment that has inappropriate printed words or images, such as foul language, suggestive topics, drugs or alcohol, gang-related messages, or Satanic words or images

As trends and fashions change, the previous rules must continue to be followed. If the fashion is to wear tops that expose the midriff, this simply is not appropriate for on the job. For men, if the fashion is for boxer shorts to be pulled up and show above the waistband of one's jeans, once again, for work this is not acceptable attire. Of course, you do not need to dress like you are much older than you are; you can wear the latest styles–if they conform to the rules. Basically, you must follow similar rules to those the children must follow. If you are not following the same rules the children are following, not only are you being a poor role model, but also you are creating a crack in the structure.

A new childcare worker at a facility for teenaged girls, Amber was a very trendy dresser. The style at the time was to wear very short skirts and shorts. Although she had been told the dress code for the facility including the fingertip test, she eventually began to slip in a pair of shorter shorts with a hooded sweatshirt, hoping no one would notice because she had dressed down the shorts. Of course the girls noticed immediately and soon were pulling out and wearing the short skirts they had in their wardrobes. One day the girls were getting ready for an outing to a movie theater. One of the girls came out in a very short skirt. Beth, one of the childcare workers on duty, asked the girl named Allie to perform the fingertip test.

"We don't have to do that anymore," Allie retorted

"Why not?" Beth asked. "It is a rule."

Allie became upset with Beth and her voice rose as she said, "It's not a rule anymore when staff wears short stuff."

"What are you talking about?"

"Amber wears short shorts all the time and no one says anything, so it's okay for us to do it, too."

Beth insisted that on her shift the rules must be followed, but Allie refused to comply. She became escalated and was kept back from the activity because her behavior was bordering on being unsafe to be in the community. Later Allie earned consequences for a verbal altercation with Beth.

The manager of the facility called Amber into his office the next day and talked to her about her clothing choices. He related to her the incident that had occurred the previous day. Amber felt horrible and never realized that bending the clothing standards for staff could cause such a problem. After that day she always followed the staff clothing guidelines.

DEMEANOR

It is important that you set a good example for your clients in terms of your demeanor while on shift. Remember your clients do not have good role models in their lives for appropriate ways to behave. They will be watching you to learn how adults carry themselves through life's variety of situations and challenges. From you and your fellow childcare workers in the milieu, they will begin to learn what it means to behave appropriately. As pointed out by Gerry Fewster (1990), "Children who are fortunate enough to learn and understand through personal encounters with adults are able to acquire the competence, confidence and knowledge to establish their own unique pathways toward self discovery, esteem, autonomy and responsibility" (p. 26).

When on shift you should always maintain a positive attitude. Your good attitude not only demonstrates to your clients an effective way to approach each day but also provides them some insight into how to approach life in general. Being positive may not be easy for you to accomplish every day. You may be having problems in your personal life or you may not be feeling well, but as we have discussed, it is vital to leave that baggage at the door and enter the facility with as upbeat an attitude as you can muster. Think again of the nurse caring for her sick patients. Imagine you are her patient. You need her to be positive and cheerful in her interactions with you as you face your own illness. A nurse with a negative attitude could make it difficult for you to have a good day, given the challenges ahead of you. The situation is exactly the same with your clients, whose emotional and psychological issues make it hard for them to have a good attitude and approach the day with positive feelings. A childcare worker with a negative attitude will make it that much more difficult for them to get through the day and work on the issues that face them.

There is plenty of research out there that suggests that a positive attitude is beneficial in all aspects of a person's health and well-being. Because many of your clients may have spent their early years being raised by a parent who was very negative, they most likely have adopted a negative attitude themselves that impedes their personal growth and development. Your positive approach to your work and your clients will show them an alternate way of behaving, and as they observe you, many clients will begin to try to emulate your attitude.

The nature of your work virtually guarantees that acting out behaviors and crisis situations will challenge your positive demeanor; however, it is helpful to remember that your clients are in your facility because of problems behaviors. The milieu therapy you provide along with counseling, psychological, and psychiatric services is designed to assist them in modifying those behaviors. Do not take their acting out personally or allow yourself to be personally affected (Harris, 2003). It will serve you well to remember that "a crucial task of the milieu is to convey to youngsters in residential treatment that signals of distress . . . will not drive the caregivers away, turn them into unreflective monsters, or hinder their ability to provide a holding, attuning, and facilitating environment" (Bleiberg, 2001, p. 251). You have an important job to do in setting limits for their behaviors, teaching them that there are consequences for inappropriate actions, and reminding them through your words and actions that you will continue to care for them even if their behavior is inappropriate or out of control. Having a positive attitude that carries throughout your shift can assist you when acting out occurs. When you feel good, it will be easier to listen to client problems and concerns, allowing them to air their feelings. You will be on your game, ready to redirect a client, interject humor when appropriate, and fairly and accurately assess a situation and clearly state choices to the client when using the PWC method. As Appelstein mentions, such interactions are most effective when your words are "delivered in a calm supportive tone of voice" (1998, p. 178). A positive attitude while on shift ensures that you will be able to maintain that appropriate composure throughout, no matter what situations come your way.

In a crisis situation, a well-maintained positive demeanor will help involved clients get through the situation and assists noninvolved clients in dealing with a situation that could be unsettling for them. Your clients probably never learned how to deal effectively with conflict or crisis. Watching you move through the incident with calmness and purposeful actions will teach them skills they can use throughout their lifetimes. Once again, earlier role models in their lives most likely showed them all the wrong ways to handle anger, conflict, and emotional upset. In addition, many television shows and movies they may watch promote the impression that the way to deal with negative emotions is through the use of physical violence, raised voices, and bad language. You will show them how to remain composed in a crisis, to mediate disputes in a reasonable yet effective fashion, and to communicate needs and feelings in ways that get the message across without physical violence, shouting, or cursing. All of this is possible when childcare workers approach their work with a calm, positive demeanor.

Remember a simple smile goes a long way and communicates volumes to a needy child. One childcare worker commented that the children at her work noticed that she was always smiling. A boy in her care asked her why. The childcare worker responded, "Because I'm happy to be here and happy to be seeing you today." The boy, trying to act tough, shrugged off her answer, but as he walked away, the childcare worker saw an obvious grin on his face.

Being positive does not mean that you should approach your work with a "Pollyanna" attitude. You should remain well aware of the serious nature of your job and the importance of the milieu therapy you provide. Do not avoid potentially volatile or difficult situations. On the contrary, you should welcome them as opportunities to teach your clients and help them through difficult times and to learn whatever you can from the experience as you become a better milieu therapist (Trieschman, 1969). As we have seen, it is your positive demeanor almost as much as any other aspect that will assist you and your clients in dealing with any situation you may face.

SPEECH

As you work with your clients, you are modeling good communication and verbal skills. Because many of our clients grew up hearing abusive and inappropriate language, learning appropriate verbal skills is critical to your clients' future successes. They must learn how to use appropriate, polite language; how to verbally deal with conflict; and how to express themselves in a manner that will facilitate their needs being met. When the children become adults, they will have to interact with employers, coworkers, doctors, apartment managers, and neighbors. Most of their communication with the people in their lives will involve the spoken word. If their language involves bad grammar, poor word choice, and slang expressions, they might not get the respect and action they deserve. You will find that many of your clients do not know how to appropriately advocate for themselves. They may not know how to ask for help or what to ask for, or they might have trouble speaking to adults or professionals.

Throughout their lives they will need to know how to appropriately express their needs in order to have them met. In the past, they may have learned all the wrong ways; now through good use of language, they can learn through your example and teaching the appropriate ways to get their needs met through verbal skills. As you interact verbally with your clients, bear in mind that you are on the front lines of teaching them good communication skills.

When you talk to your clients, you should always use appropriate language. Never

1. Use curse words
2. Raise your voice or yell at a client (The only exception is if the client is in immediate danger or at immediate risk of harm.)
3. Resort to name calling or personal insult
4. Order a client to do anything (except if a client is in imminent danger)

Your clients must be spoken to with respect and politeness at all times. You will quickly find that if you show your clients respect and politeness your clients will treat you the same much of the time. In most states, it is considered a violation of a child's personal rights to speak to them in a raised voice or to yell at them. Children in residential placement have the right to be spoken to in a calm appropriate manner and never to be addressed in a loud, disrespectful manner.

You will quickly find that ordering a child to do something does not get you anywhere. Instead, it may engage you in an immediate and unintended power struggle with that child. This is especially true when working with children who are diagnosed with oppositional defiant disorder. For them, the command spells untrustworthy authority figure, and they will respond with disrespect or even anger and likely will not complete the directive presented to them. A much better approach is to ask them to do something–never demand. Giving the child a choice to do or not to do what you have asked is empowering and casts you in a different light in their eyes. You are not a negative authority figure demanding action; instead you are someone who respects his or her right to choose. More often than not, asking a child to do something will result in a choice of action that will be positive for everyone. In addition, you are modeling for children an appropriate and effective way to have their needs met. After many interactions, many children will begin to recognize it is better to ask than to demand and to respect the right of others to choose.

One tool you may find especially useful is to be polite and nondemanding in all of your interactions with your clients. As we have seen, the use of "I" statements works very well, but even further than that, just as a smile goes a long way, as does a sprinkling of "please" and "thank you" (Appelstein, 1998). Using these words says, "I respect you, care about your feelings, and appreciate you and your efforts." For children with oppositional defiant disorder you move from being an overbearing authority figure to someone who asks for a cooperative effort. As you verbally interact with your clients in this way, you are teaching them how to communicate effectively. If you reward them with praise when they say please or thank you, the message will be communicated more strongly. Do not be surprised if you hear your clients mimicking your use of good language. In addition, many childcare workers also let clients know they are sorry in a variety of situations, from having to give consequences to personally making an error and/or to expressing empathy. Your expression of regret shows that you care and are considerate in the actions you take regarding your clients (Appelstein, 1998). You are modeling how to express oneself in different situations and sending the message that it is okay to be wrong or to have to do something one may not like because it is the responsible thing to do.

Many times new childcare workers do not know how to use their words to role model and teach appropriate communication while eliciting from the children the desired responses. You may have some instruction in this regard during your initial training, but for the most part, no one really teaches this stuff. Parents certainly could use the instruction but have little time to access the information even if they could find it. In your work, good communication with your clients is critical to your success. Sometimes the easiest way to see the right way is to understand the wrong way. Let us look at some examples of language mistakes and how to improve them.

Example 1

Problem: Tommy, come over here and pick up your toys now.
Better: *Tommy, could you please come over and help me pick up the toys?*

In this example, the childcare worker is literally ordering the child to pick up his toys with the ending zinger "now." The communication comes off very bossy and authoritarian. A childcare worker who communicates with children in this way is not likely to earn their respect and cooperation; indeed, she may hear the children actually telling her she is bossy or worse. In the improved version, the worker asks the child not only to pick up the toys, but also to help *her* pick them up. In the better version, it is not a chore for the child, but rather helping out the childcare worker with a task she has. Much more cooperation, especially from younger children, will result from this approach.

Example 2

Problem: Jodie, put away the milk before it gets spoiled.
Better: *Hey, Jodie, I need you to put away the milk, please. We don't want it to get spoiled.*

Here we again see the childcare worker ordering the child to do something, although the command is somewhat softened. The improved version uses an "I" statement that does not order the client but instead requests an action using the word "please," modeling politeness and showing respect for the child. Finally, a reason is given for performing the action and includes the child in the desire to have the milk not spoil by using the word "we."

Example 3

Problem: I wrote down the wrong thing on your chart yesterday.
Better: *Molly, I'm so sorry I made a mistake on your chart yesterday. I'll fix it right away.*

Although the first sentence is good in that it does admit that a mistake was made, which shows children that adult authority figures are human, make mistakes, and can admit to them, the statement does not go far enough. The better version addresses the child by name, targeting the words just for her, and then goes on to not just admit the mistake but also apologize for the mistake. Not only is the mistake noticed and an apology offered, but also a promise is made to correct the mistake immediately. What a lovely model for children to learn appropriate communication in a difficult situation.

Example 4

Problem: I've checked and see that your chore is done. I'll make a note of it.
Better: *Thank you for doing your chore. I really appreciate it.*

The first example here is bland and emotionless and misses an important opportunity to acknowledge the child's accomplishments. The better example repairs this by offering thanks and appreciation for the child's efforts. Imagine the child smiling after hearing the better example or walking off to his room with no reaction or disappointment when hearing the first part of the example.

Example 5

Problem: Well, everybody gets picked on. Don't let it bother you.
Better: *I'm so sorry this is happening to you. Maybe we can think of some ways to help you get through it.*

Overall, notice how the first sentences in this example seem to write off the child's concerns and do little to acknowledge the child's feelings. It is much better to express that you feel concern that the child is feeling badly and are offering a helping hand if the child wants to take it. The better example shows concern for the child's needs and feelings. Children will react to this show of empathy and from it begin to learn to feel and express empathy for others. Rather than "writing off" the child's concerns, the second approach offers to find some solutions to help the child work through the problem.

Taking every opportunity to verbally thank and/or praise your clients for their efforts, however small, helps to build their self-esteem and lets them know their efforts are appreciated and do not go unnoticed. Children who were raised in environments where they rarely received positive feedback from adults are literally hungry for that acknowledgment. In addition, verbally praising your clients for talents and abilities or just doing a good job in any arena helps to make them feel good about themselves. As suggested in the previous chapter, make it a practice to verbally praise each of your clients at least two times per shift.

In order to maintain appropriate speech with your clients, you will need to have your professional demeanor strong and functioning. You will need to remain calm, so that you can use your words appropriately. If you lose your cool you risk not communicating effectively and appropriately. It is important that your choice of tone and words is measured and carefully controlled, especially during a potentially volatile situation. In your work, you should never fight fire with fire or you will have an explosion on your hands. An emotionally disturbed child will react to angry, loud, or demanding language or tone of voice in kind and then some (Trieschman, 1969) You can easily escalate an already emotionally troubled child through inappropriate communication, but you can just as easily diffuse and de-escalate through appropriate use of language and tone of voice. You will find that the first avenue to de-escalating a crisis is through calm, measured, verbal communication.

Using slang is usually not a good idea, especially if you are trying to use the vocabulary that young people use. Children, especially teenagers, will recognize very quickly that you are attempting to be something you are not, and children do not respect childcare workers when they think are being phony. A better choice is to use good grammar and avoid slang words and expressions. As you use good grammar and language skills you are modeling appropriate communication for your client. These skills will be important for them now and for the rest of their lives.

AUTHORITY

Because the children in your care did not have effective parenting in their lives before entering treatment, an important part of your work is modeling what it is to be a positive authority figure. As we have already seen, your clients do not need more friends; they need positive adults to care for them, keep them safe, and set limits and boundaries within which they can function and work on their emotional, behavioral, and psychological issues.

Many of the children in your care have difficulty dealing with authority figures because the adults who were supposed to care for them did not do a suitable job or even caused them harm. It is only natural that they do not trust adults in positions of authority; however, as they grow toward adulthood that mistrust can cause many problems and difficulties for them. As a childcare worker, you have a duty to show your clients that authority figures can be trusted and can do what must be done to care for them, protect them, and teach them how to be productive adults. For many of your clients, this will not be easy to accomplish, so deep is their hurt and mistrust, but as with so many of their issues, doing your part will contribute to the whole of the treatment and therapy they will receive throughout their childhoods and beyond. You may not see a marked difference. You may never hear them thank you for your efforts. Nevertheless, you can make a difference, however small, for most if not all of the children in your care as part of the complete picture of the treatment they will receive throughout their lives. In many cases, affecting a client's view of authority figures could be among the most important work you do. The effect is cumulative, happening in little ways on every shift you work.

Some of the children you work with may already be diagnosed with oppositional defiant disorder, which is characterized by a serious mistrust of authority figures. Considering their histories, it is no surprise that these children do not trust adult authority figures. After all, the adults they trusted most hurt them and failed to meet their needs for protection and security. Although oppositional defiant disorder can sometimes be difficult for adults to deal with, particularly in school settings where teachers may not be trained to deal with such a disorder. The real problem comes when the disorder is not addressed. Left untreated, this disorder can progress to a conduct disorder, which essentially takes oppositional defiant disorder to a level of disregard for authority that results in engaging in criminal behaviors. From there, a few may move to an antisocial personality disorder, which essentially means they have no regard for authority or empathy for others and no remorse for habitual criminal behavior. Your efforts to be a positive authority figure can assist your client in learning that authority figures can be trusted and do care about them. You can literally be a part of making a difference that helps to save your clients from a lifetime of one incarceration after another.

In order to be a positive authority figure in their lives, there are some areas to which you should pay particular attention:

1. Concern for client needs
2. Making the hard decisions
3. Fairness
4. Follow through
5. Reward

CONCERN FOR CLIENT NEEDS

You may already have recognized that your clients have many and varied needs. Earlier in their lives, their medical needs may have been neglected or they may not have been given the proper nutrition. Adults in their lives may not have cared to listen when they were upset or anxious. They may never have truly felt safe. Now that they are your clients, it is important that through your actions you send the message that you do care and that their needs will be heard and attended to in a timely manner.

You may demonstrate this in small ways, such as getting them a cotton swab when they request one or a fresh bar of soap when they have run out. You can also send this message in larger ways, such as listening with an empathetic ear when they talk about their anxieties or making sure to note a medical complaint and having an appointment made to see a doctor. Everyday over and over, you and your fellow staff members attend to their needs as a way of making them see that authority figures do what they are supposed to do, are worthy of respect, and can be valuable in their lives (Maier, 1990).

Do not take this lightly. Whenever clients make a request for your time, attention, and assistance, you must be available to help. If you are busy with other tasks, let your clients know that you will be able assist them as soon as possible, unless the need is immediate. In fact, it sends a good message to show them that although you are there to be of service, you are not at their beck and call at all times, which does not engender respect. However, if you cannot get to the request right away, give the client a time frame and follow through. If you cannot, apologize and give an estimation of when you will be available to help or ask a coworker to attend to the task.

Do not make the mistake of forgetting that you are a part of a team. You are not the be-all and end-all for any client. As just mentioned, ask another childcare worker to assist you if you cannot follow through in a timely manner because of other responsibilities. Sometimes you will want to let the client know that you will call on another staff person who is better equipped to handle the issue. For example, if a client needs to see a doctor for a medical concern, tell the client that you will leave a note for the staff person responsible for making doctor appointments so that he or she can take care of it. Sometimes clients will talk to you about past traumas in great detail. It is okay to listen empathetically, but you should at some point let them know that they need to discuss the matter with their therapist or your facility's social worker. Tell them that you will leave a note for the appropriate therapist to make sure he or she is aware. When clients discuss problems with school, let them know that they should talk to the staff person in charge of that aspect of their treatment. Once again, inform them that you will leave a note alerting the appropriate staff to the problem. Remember you are just a part of the client's overall care at your facility and are not expected to do everything. Your clients' needs are so great and varied that it takes an entire staff to care for them all. The important thing to get across to your clients, however, is that they have been heard and that someone who can best serve them will handle the matter.

MAKING THE HARD DECISIONS

Oftentimes parents and adult authority figures have to make hard decisions in order to protect, care for, and educate children. As a childcare worker, you will often be called upon to make those hard decisions. Part of your job will be to say no in the face of the disappointment your client will no doubt experience. Doing this is difficult for many childcare workers, but you can become more accustomed to the obligation if you have a clear understanding of the importance of your role as an authority figure in your clients' life. Your clients actually need and want the boundaries that you set for their behavior by setting a limit for their behavior. Without the safety and security of the limits and boundaries of your program and the limits you set as a childcare worker, children in residential care would begin to feel unsafe and acting out behaviors would start for many of them. Indeed, most of the time you will find that even if your clients complain or cry when told they cannot do something, they will respect your position and eventually accept your answer. Although they would never admit it, they appreciate the parental role of setting limits being filled in their lives, perhaps for the first time. The children will learn from you what it means to be a responsible adult authority figure as they watch you set limits in a calm, responsible manner.

Many times it is difficult to exercise your role as an authority figure by setting limits for a client's behavior and having to give consequences. Giving consequences and informing the client are especially difficult when a client are already escalated, upset, and angry. However if you follow the PWC method outlined in Chapter 6–give a *prompt,* followed by a *warning,* and then follow through with a *consequence* if the behavior persists–you will find it much easier to do. When clients receive a prompt and a warning, you are giving them the choice to change their behavior as well as clearly informing them what will happen if they choose to continue. In doing so, you give them some power in the situation. You are still the person in authority, but you are working to give them a choice to avoid the consequence. Once again, when you have to say no or give a consequence, it is okay to express your regret in having to do so. In this way, the client gets the message that you are not one who enjoys taking things away, and that you would rather not have to do so.

Being overly permissive does not protect a child or teach appropriate behavior. Children do not feel safe in such an environment. Making the hard choices and taking the heat makes you a good role model for an adult authority figure. You do not like it either, but in the child's best interest it has to be done. The children will notice this and learn more from your role modeling what being an adult, a parent, and a person in authority is really all about.

FAIRNESS

In order to role model authority effectively, you must be fair in all of your dealings with your clients. Your treatment of your clients must be equal. No playing favorites, no allowing to one client some freedom and not another. You must strive at all times to be just in your application of rules and consequences, policies and procedures, and praise and rewards. In addition, you should make an effort to spend equal time with all clients whenever you are on shift. If you do not practice fairness and equality with your clients, your credibility as an authority figure will be diminished. The negative view your clients have of authority figures will be reinforced.

You must be aware of your need to practice fairness at all times while on shift. Here are some suggestions to keep it fair:

1. Plan to spend at least fifteen minutes with each client on every shift whenever possible.
2. Know the rules and consequences well, be constantly vigilant for violations, and be sure to use the PWC method.
3. Praise each client at least two times while you are on shift.
4. Try to reward each client at least one time each shift whenever possible using your facility's reward system.
5. If accused of being unfair by a client, carefully listen to the complaint, and if the complaint is valid, apologize to the client and talk to your supervisor about ways to reconcile the situation.

Sometimes in a facility full of children it may be difficult to spend time with each of them. In fact, most childcare workers do not make an effort to do so, preferring to interact with the children in groups or even to spend the most time with the children they like better than the others. Practicing and maintaining fairness takes effort, and setting the goal of spending fifteen minutes on each shift with each child is a good way to consciously add the concern of fairness to your work. You do not have to corner each child and demand his or her attention; that may be intimidating. Instead, look for naturally occurring opportunities. For example, if you see Ethan playing alone with a toy truck, go over and play with him. Ask him how things are going at school or how his last visit with his father went. When the boys are taking a walk with you and other staff, you might walk up to Caleb and tell him how proud you are of his recent turnaround in behavior. If fifteen-year-old Margie is preparing a dinner she selected for the rest of the girls and staff, you might go into the kitchen, help her chop some vegetables, and talk about whatever she has on her mind. The possibilities are endless, and you will see them when you are consciously looking.

Knowing the rules well and being on the lookout for violations is important to keeping it fair. If you let things slide one day and are on top of the rules another day, you are modeling inconsistency and unfairness. Think about the image of an authority figure you are sending to the girl who broke a rule yesterday and received consequences as she watches you let seemingly ignore another girl violating the same rule today—just because you are not paying as much attention. Being vigilant does not mean slamming the children for every little rule violation. This is where the PWC method comes in handy. Most times you will find children will comply in the prompt stage.

Praising your client, as we have seen, is an important part of raising their self-esteem and showing them that good behavior is rewarded. In order to role model an authority figure who is fair, you must make an effort to be equal in your praise to all of the children in your care. Setting the goal of praising each at least two times every shift will keep you on track for being a role model of an authority figure who is fair and treats all of the children equally.

Trying to reward each child one time per shift using your facility's system of rewards is another important way you can demonstrate a balanced authority figure. You will give consequences when you need to set a limit, but you will also reward good behavior. Again, you must be fair in your dispensing of rewards. That is why setting the goal of rewarding each child one time works well. Often the reward, using your facility's system of rewards, will naturally follow the praise that you are focusing on giving to each of your clients.

Children in residential treatment are constantly on the lookout for things that are unfair on the part of childcare workers. When you are accused of an instance of unfairness, do not be alarmed. Sit down with the client and carefully listen to the complaint. If the complaint appears valid or has any degree of validity, acknowledge that to the client and apologize. Then clearly state to the client how you will remedy the situation. You may need to talk to your supervisor to get advice on how to remedy the situation if it goes beyond what you are authorized to do; for example, you may not be authorized to cancel removal of privileges for a rule violation because only a supervisor can do that. If you need to talk your supervisor before reaching a resolution with your client, be sure to let the client know this by telling her or him that you will carefully explain the error that you have made to your boss. You are role modeling for your client that authority figures are big enough to face up to and admit their mistakes, apologize for them, and correct them. Doing these things makes an authority figure seem more human and approachable.

FOLLOW THROUGH

When working with children, it is imperative that you say what you mean and mean what you say. If you tell a child you are going to do something, you must follow through and do it. A child in placement learns very quickly when a childcare worker does not always do what he or she says and will know instinctively that childcare worker can be manipulated and does not have to be taken seriously. The next time he or she gives children a prompt or a warning it will be almost meaningless. He or she has lost their attention and their respect.

If you prompt children and/or give a warning, you must follow through with what you have said you are going to do in response to the choice they make. They may not like the consequences, but because you have followed through they will remember the next time and probably choose to attempt to control or eliminate the problem behavior. They will understand that you mean what you say and there is no room for manipulation. You will have earned their respect.

The same is also true if you do not follow through with a task you have promised to a client. The child may lose trust in you and possibly the whole program. He or she may become anxious and fear that his or her needs are not going to be met. For example, ten-year-old Jimmy told childcare worker Lloyd that his wrist had been hurting for several days. Jimmy was new to the program and still wondered if it was a safe place for him. Lloyd promised Jimmy that he would leave a note for his supervisor, who was responsible for making doctor appointments. Several hours later Lloyd finished his shift and left for the day without writing the note. The next few days Jimmy waited and did not hear anything about an appointment to examine his wrist being scheduled. The wrist pain continued and got worse. Jimmy began to distrust Lloyd and other staff by association. Finally, after three days Jimmy told his county social worker about what had happened. The supervisor got an earful from the county social worker, and Lloyd was reprimanded. Fortunately, Jimmy's therapist was able to convince him to give the staff another chance to earn his trust.

Sometimes childcare workers, especially those new to the field, are eager to please the children with whom they work and will sometimes make promises that they are unlikely to keep or be able to keep. Making false promises to children role models poor behavior by an authority figure. It may also trigger painful memories of promises their parents made to them but failed to keep. For example, many children who come from families with drug and alcohol addiction have had their parents promise over and over again that they would stop drinking or using drugs. These children saw those promises unfulfilled and watched as their lives crumbled. A childcare worker who promises to take the children to an amusement park before asking his supervisor if such a trip is feasible is making promises to the children he probably will not be able to keep. Better to stick with your facility's program and clear any special ideas for treats and outings with your supervisor before discussing anything about them with the children.

REWARD

A positive authority figure does not simply set limits, make hard decisions, and hand out consequences. He also had a softer side, one that praises and rewards good behavior. This is important for your clients because as Trieschman (1969) writes,

> Unlike normal children, these children have not learned to associate adults with pleasant experiences; they have not found that adults meet their needs in predictable ways, nor can adults be counted on in times of trouble. More likely they have learned that adults are connected with unpleasant circumstances. . . . (p. 66)

As you reward your clients and show your softer side, you are helping them to unlearn their negative view of authority figures.

Children learn as much if not more from praise and reward as they do from consequence, so an authority figure must be generous in handing out recognition for good behavior and accomplishment. If all you do is give out negative feedback, you are the kind of authority figure they have learned to dislike and mistrust. If you can show them you appreciate their positive attributes and deeds, however, you are the kind of adult they can trust and even like to be around.

If you are always criticizing and handing out consequences, your clients will be reluctant to approach you, but if you praise and reward them for good behavior, clients will want to interact with you. It is okay to have fun with the children in your care, to play, laugh, and joke with them as well. You will find if you do so, children will be more eager to open up to you and trust you to meet their needs and keep them safe. You are a real person—an adult who can have a good time with them and acknowledge positive behaviors and accomplishments, but who also maintains his or her authority, which you will use when necessary.

Rewarding your clients will show them that adult authority figures are not to be mistrusted or even feared as they may have learned in the past. The new view you are giving them will help them become more comfortable with all adults in authority—no small accomplishment provided by your milieu therapy.

CHAPTER 8 REVIEW

1. Most of the children in residential treatment have had few positive role models in their lives. Childcare workers have a unique opportunity to be positive role models for these children.

2. Positive role modeling encompasses much of the childcare worker's time while on shift and is part of every interaction the childcare worker has with the children.

3. Childcare workers should model appropriate appearance for their clients, always presenting as professional and polished, while being dressed and groomed for whatever activities are planned.

4. In a residential setting, childcare workers are constantly looked upon by the children as models for acceptable demeanor. Through watching childcare workers, children learn how healthy adults carry themselves in life's many situations and challenges.

5. A childcare worker should always maintain a positive attitude while on shift, giving children insight in how to approach life. Personal problems and issues must not be taken to work. Just like a nurse must maintain her bedside manner to help patients who are sick and in pain, the childcare worker needs the same when interacting with children in care. This is especially true during crisis situations where a positive attitude will assist in maintaining calm and clarity of thought and action.

6. Role modeling positive speech assists children in learning good communication and verbal skills. Childcare workers should never use curse words, raise their voices or yell at a client, resort to name calling or personal insult, or order a client to do anything. Clients should always be spoken to with respect and politeness.

7. Because many of the children in care were so let down and even abused by the adults in their lives, they are mistrustful of authority figures. Childcare workers must role model positive use of authority. Above all childcare workers must show a concern for their clients' needs while on shift.

8. Childcare workers are often called upon to make the hard decisions that adults caring for children must make. Sometimes they must give consequences and remove privileges when setting limits for a child's behavior. The child may become angry or upset, but the positive authority figure is able to do what is in the child's best interest and take the heat for it.

9. Above all, a positive authority figure is fair in all dealings with clients. All must be treated equally. In order to ensure fairness, try spending at least fifteen minutes with each client on each shift. Know the rules and consequences and use the PWC method. Try to praise each child at least two times per shift. Reward each child at least one time on every shift. Handle complaints professionally.

10. Follow-through is a very important aspect of positive authority. Never threaten children or say things they know you cannot accomplish. Only say what you are willing and able to do.

11. A positive authority figure rewards children for good behaviors. He or she is not solely concerned with handing out consequences.

EXERCISE

When it comes to being a positive role model for children, we all have our strengths as well as areas where we could use some extra work. For this exercise, write down five strengths you have as a role model and how you use each of these strengths to benefit your clients. Then jot down five areas where you feel that your presentation as a positive role model could be improved and then describe how you plan to improve in each.

Strengths

1. Strength:

   Benefits:

2. Strength:

   Benefits:

3. Strength:

   Benefits:

4. Strength:

   Benefits:

5. Strength:

   Benefits:

Weaknesses

1. Needs Improvement:

   Plan:

2. Needs Improvement:

   Plan:

3. Needs Improvement:

   Plan:

4. Needs Improvement:

   Plan:

5. Needs Improvement:

   Plan:

Chapter 9

ELEMENTS OF MILIEU THERAPY: CONSISTENCY

In your work as a milieu therapist, it is very important that you maintain consistency throughout every shift. Consistency means uniformity in all aspects of your job. Your clients need consistency in order to feel safe. After experiencing the chaos of their early lives, the children in your care need the stability your facility provides and the consistent work of each childcare worker. Consistency offers certainty. Within that certainty, children can begin to address their issues and problems with the assistance of your facility's staff. The children at your facility will relax knowing that they can expect a calm environment where limits are set for their behavior and all their needs are met. As a childcare worker, maintaining consistency results in your shifts being more orderly and manageable, making your work easier over all. Staying consistent is a win-win for both the children and the childcare workers.

In order to maintain consistency, you must strive to be the same and approach your work the same way every time you are on shift. Children in care quickly learn how a consistently run shift will run and will settle into the routine; in fact, they will come to expect and enjoy it. Consistency encompasses all of the elements of milieu therapy that have been discussed in preceding chapters. Each, however, is worth revisiting, specifically with an eye to maintaining consistency. The next chapter will detail another important way to maintain consistency—effective communication among staff. In both written and verbal communication, childcare workers must "be on the same page" or consistency may be lost.

PROGRAM STRUCTURE

Because program structure is the most important component of milieu therapy, the success of your consistent approach depends on your ability to uniformly and regularly enforce the program structure. You must always use and apply your program's rules, consequences, and reward systems. The children will view you as fair and respectable if you consistently apply the rules to all children equally. Remember that children are on the lookout for situations that seem unfair, so they will be the first to catch you if you are inconsistent in your application of your program's rules and consequences. Take this as a learning experience, reread the rules and consequences, and strive to do better the next time.

In all situations you must adhere to your facility's policies and procedures. The polices and procedures exist to form the way the program functions therapeutically. For example, your program's rules, consequences, and rewards systems are all segments of policies and procedures. Independent living skills activities for older children compose another aspect of the therapeutic program. When your program was conceived, the policies and procedures were carefully constructed in order to provide children with an effective learning and growing environment where their treatment needs are met most effectively. Upper management in well-run facilities are periodically looking for ways to improve policies and procedures, so in programs that have existed for five years or more there have likely been several improvements to improve this important aspect of program structure. Do not be surprised if you find a change in policy or procedure introduced at a staff meeting or in a memo. Although some childcare workers might resist, if it represents an enhancement to your existing program, the change is a good thing and has been well-planned and thought out. Nevertheless, supervisors will be carefully watching to test the effectiveness of the new practices and will welcome the feedback of childcare workers, who after all are the ones who know best how well the new practice is working. You will find that management will be receptive to suggestions and feedback whenever something new is introduced and will take your comments seriously.

Uppermost in your mind should be to follow the house schedule and never deviate without the permission of your supervisor. As we have seen, the house schedule becomes the backbone program day to day. In essence, all other aspects of program structure rest upon the house schedule. Children rely on the house schedule because it lets them know what will happen that day, and this gives them a greater sense of security. Routine is so important for children, especially children who have gone through periods of their lives where there was none. The house schedule sets the routine that children need each day. Some facilities find that posting a schedule for an entire week works well for them. This works well for older children but may be too much to digest for younger children. Other facilities post the schedule for a couple of days so that children will know what to expect in days to come. Whatever procedure your facility uses for the house schedule, make sure that you are consistently keyed in to that schedule and follow it religiously.

At all times while on shift, you must maintain your professional demeanor. In order to maintain consistency, you must leave your troubles, worries, aches, pains, and upsets at the door and enter the facility like a nurse ready to tend to sick patients with an upbeat and cheerful attitude. If you allow your personal issues to mix with your job, you will find it difficult to be consistent when enforcing the program structure. With a lot happening on shift and much to keep track of, you must be on top of your game. Remember, a smile goes a long way when working with troubled children.

In order to grow in your role as a childcare worker, you must listen carefully to the direction and counsel of your supervisors and seek them out for assistance when you have a problem or concern. Your supervisors will be able to help you with useful advice and suggestions. Especially when you are new to the field or new to a facility, you will need to rely on seasoned staff and supervisors to help you be consistent as you are learning. In many instances, it is best to take a back seat to staff members who have more experience than you do, especially when dealing with a crisis. Although there is a lot of information for new staff to digest related to a program's structure, all will eventually take shape. In order to avoid being inconsistent when you are first starting as a childcare worker or are beginning work at a new program, it is best to defer to senior staff in situations where you are uncertain. Also important is frequent and regular communication with your immediate supervisor to gauge your progress and get feedback on how to improve your consistency on the job.

HOUSE SCHEDULE

Consistency within the milieu depends on all childcare workers' following the house schedule, which forms the backbone of your program structure. As we have seen, the house schedule tells your clients what will happen every day and communicates that their needs will be met each and every day. The house schedule helps them feel safe and cared for. Following the house schedule lets the children know that childcare workers will follow through with what they say.

The quickest way to fail to achieve consistency in your work is not following the house schedule. All it takes is one day of deviating from the schedule or even one instance on one day to send a message to children that staff cannot be trusted to do what they are supposed to do. This begs the question in even the latency-aged child: "If she doesn't do what she is supposed to, why should I?" When you do not adhere to the schedule, your clients begin to wonder what they can count on at your facility. If you are the only one not following the schedule, you can imagine the confusion clients will experience because other staff recognize the importance of the schedule and use it as a road map for the day. Emotionally disturbed children are especially affected by this particular inconsistency and acting our behaviors will almost certainly occur, especially in younger children.

The house schedule is perhaps the easiest area in which to maintain consistency. It is there, clearly posted, and contains the hour by hour details of the day. Following the schedule is elementary, yet so important to the program and children in care. Unfortunately, because many childcare workers do not understand its importance, the house schedule is a place where inconsistency among staff members happens most frequently.

BOUNDARIES

Remaining consistent in maintaining good boundaries is critical to good practice as a professional childcare worker. You must never share sensitive personal information with your clients and refrain from sharing details about your life with them. You do not know how clients will receive sensitive personal information, but above all, your personal information takes the focus off the clients. Focus must always remain on the clients and their needs. Arrive for each shift comfortable with your role as an authority figure in your clients' lives. Do not try to be their friend. The children in your care do not need more friends. They need caring adult authority figures who will make sure their needs are met, set limits for their behavior, and keep them safe. Do not act outside your scope of practice. Any activity that would require a license or certification to perform outside of the house is not within the scope of a childcare worker's job. Avoid playing favorites. Take steps on every shift to be as fair and equal in your treatment of each child as possible. Be vigilant of what could be a developing rescue fantasy.

Operating on shift with a rescue fantasy virtually guarantees that you will not be able to be consistent. Remember that your role in a child's treatment is only one small piece of the pie that represents the treatment he or she has received, is receiving, and will receive in the future. No one person can take care all your clients' many treatment needs.

To be sure that you are maintaining consistent boundaries on shift, seek out your supervisor for her or his evaluation of how you are doing. It is valuable to get that kind of feedback because you may not be aware that your boundaries are becoming inconsistent or going astray. Talking to your coworkers will also give you valuable feedback on your consistency. Having open lines of communication with your peers is important in so many ways, as we will see, and it can be very helpful in keeping each other on track from day to day and shift to shift when it comes to consistency. Be open to feedback from coworkers, and when you offer feedback to others try to frame it in a constructive manner. We will cover this in depth in the chapter on communication.

SETTING LIMITS

Know the rules and consequences well and apply them fairly, evenly, and equally among your clients. Because your list of rules and consequences may be long, it is okay to refer to them when faced with an incidence of rule violation. Be sure to use the PWC method whenever possible. When you see a rule violation, first issue a prompt for the behavior to stop. If the behavior continues, give a warning that details precisely what consequences will be given if the behavior continues. Finally, if the behavior still does not stop, you must follow through with the consequences detailed in the warning. Follow-through is critical. If you become identified as a staff person who does not follow through, you will begin to be viewed as a pushover and will see an increase in acting out behavior and manipulation on your shift. Consistency will be lost. When setting limits, make certain to use "I" statements. "I" statements soften the message and make the limit setting less accusatory. Also, it is recommended that the rules and consequences be treated as a separate entity that you must follow as part of your job; good practice also involves the emphasizing of choice in any rule violation. The PWC method is very helpful in that regard, but you can also express regret that your client made the choice he or she made that resulted in your having to give consequences. All of these techniques work to ensure that setting limits is consistent and fair.

While on shift you must avoid power struggles with your clients. You will not win a power struggle with a child in treatment. They are far better at it than you are. A power struggle with a client is likely to change the mood of the entire house from positive to negative in very short order. When engaged in a power struggle with a client, you are treating that child differently than you treat the others, and your focus must remain on that child for the duration of the encounter. As you can see, the power struggle gets you nowhere and threatens your ability to be consistent. Unfortunately, it is easy to get pulled into a power struggle. You must be constantly vigilant and rely on the feedback and signals of your coworkers in order to steer clear of them and maintain your consistent approach to your work.

Be aware of your clients' tendency to test limits and manipulate. Maintain good communication with coworkers while on shift to ensure that you are not being tested or manipulated. Children in treatment will try to split staff or engage staff or staff shop. Solid communication among staff on shift will circumvent these types of manipulation and help you to maintain consistency.

REWARDING POSITIVE BEHAVIOR

Make sure to consistently reward all of your clients for positive behaviors. It is so important to reward children, especially children in residential care. Those children may never have been consistently rewarded for good behavior. They may have given up on being "good" children. When you reward them, you are showing them that it feels good to be good. Rewards for positive behavior and accomplishments help to build a child's self esteem. When you give rewards, you are showing children that adult authority figures do not simply dole out consequences but also recognize the good and acknowledge it.

When considering rewarding clients, be well-versed in your facility's system for giving rewards or consequences. Whether it is progress toward moving up a behavioral level or points that will increase a child's allowance, childcare workers must be watching for opportunities to give reward. Sometimes childcare workers become too focused on negative behavior and miss opportunities to reward clients. A realization of how important reward is will help in those instances. Although both reward and consequence are necessary aspects of residential treatment, most executive directors will agree that more progress is made through reward than through consequence. Above all, you must be consistent in rewarding your clients and not showing favoritism in the rewards you give. The children in your care will be on the lookout for inconsistencies and will quickly bring it to your attention if you are not being equal in the way you reward clients.

Praise is one of the easiest and most direct ways to reward children's behavior. Children respond so favorably to verbal positive reinforcement of their behavior. A good way to maintain praise consistency is to endeavor to praise each client at least two times on every shift. Remember, the children who are the most difficult to praise are the ones who need your praise the most.

Be aware of each client's baseline behavior so that you can be consistent in rewarding positive behavior in a way that is realistic and probable for every individual client. Using baselines allows you to praise children according to their abilities. Without baselines some children would rarely perform to a level that would warrant praise or reward. For these children, the baseline provides a realistic representation of their abilities that allows you to reward the small things. Do not be surprised as you watch the rewards for the small things make a big difference in the progress of a child toward his or her treatment goals.

ROLE MODELING

Remember that role modeling appropriate behavior is a large part of milieu therapy. Children in your care learn from seeing your behavior and appearance. They may never have been exposed to positive adults in their young lives. The responsibility to be a positive role model is not to be taken lightly. Taken seriously, role modeling can become one of the easiest ways consistency can be maintained. Be consistent in presenting yourself as a positive model of behavior at all times.

As you have seen, several key factors come into play in being a good role model for your clients. First, you must consistently present yourself as appropriately attired and well-groomed. You should at the very least follow the same clothing rules that the children must follow. Nothing undermines consistency faster than when staff wear clothing the children would not be permitted to wear. Take care to dress in clothing that is appropriate for the activities scheduled for each shift. Check the schedule for upcoming events on your next shift. You do not want to come to work in dress shoes when hiking in a local park is planned.

Second, an imperative for good role modeling is to maintain a positive demeanor while on shift. You should be perceived as being the same on every shift you work. Never should your clients comment that some days you are in a good mood but other days you are grouchy. If clients are talking about your varying moods, you have failed to leave your personal baggage at the door. As a result, when you arrived for work your demeanor was inconsistent from one shift to the next. Keep in mind nurses caring for sick patients. Think of the demeanor you would wish them to have were they caring for you. That is the way you should present yourself to your clients.

Third, on every shift you must consistently use good language skills in your communications with your clients. Never raise your voice, use curse words, or resort to name calling. Always use good grammar and avoid slang words and expressions. In your communication with your clients you should always keep the focus on them. Your work is all about them. Do not order a child to do anything (except when there is a safety issue involved). Instead, ask the client. In this way you are giving the child choice and empowering him or her. The use of "I" statements is also important. By using "I" statements you are taking the accusatory or blaming aspect out of your words and modeling appropriate communication skills. The children in your care have had plenty of models of poor communication in their lives. Television shows they may watch also highlight poor communication skills. It is up to you to show them the right way to communicate, which is so important to their ability to get along with others.

Finally, consistently be a positive authority figure as you model how a positive adult cares for, protects, and sets limits for children. To maintain your position as a positive role model in your clients' lives, you will need to bear in mind a few specific suggestions. Make concern and caring for your clients' needs a priority. Strive to be there for them and meet their needs. You may be among the first in their lives who has done this for them. When they feel cared for, children feel safe. In essence, you are creating the nest of safety from which they will be able not only to work on their issues but also to simply be kids and have fun.

As a positive authority figure, you must be able to make the hard decisions that adults often have to make when taking care of children. You will be called upon to set limits for behavior and give consequences even when you know a child might cry or be angry with you. In other instances, you will have to say no quite a bit. Children will ask for things that simply are not permitted, such as an unscheduled trip to get ice cream or being allowed to watch television when on loss of television privileges. Here again you will make the children unhappy in the short term in your role as an authority figure. However, your parental role with the children demands that you "take the heat" in the interest of creating a safe and consistent environment for them. In the end, the children will respect you for it and may even think back to how staff handled situations when they are raising their own children.

Always be fair in your application of policies, procedures, rules, consequences, and rewards. Children in care are constantly on the lookout for favoritism or unevenness in following all of your facility's policies and procedures. If you are showing favoritism to one or more children, the other children will recognize it and complain or even begin acting out. Fairness in all that you do should be uppermost in your mind while on shift. You can show children that authority figures can be fair in their role. In this way, you will begin to teach children that authority figures are not always to be mistrusted or even feared. Instead, authority figures can actually be positives in their lives.

Whenever you tell a client you are going to do something, follows through with what you have told them. Lack of follow-through will be seen as a sign of weakness and children will quickly learn they can get away with things when you are on shift. Positive authority figures say what they mean and mean what they say. When using the PWC method, follow-through is an imperative. The method does work, but only if there is follow through. Once again, you will be showing children how effective parents do their job, and although you may never know it, a child in your care may think back to the example you set when raising their own children. You may be among the first to model good parenting for the children in your care.

Take care to regularly and consistently reward clients for good behavior and accomplishments. Positive authority figures are not merely taskmasters meting out consequences. Instead, positive authority figures can be generous in praise and reward. Many children are surprised to find that authority figures can even be fun. At a local fair for children, a booth was dedicated to canine officers and their dogs. There were several beautiful police dogs and their handlers. Knowing children loved dogs, childcare worker Patty encouraged the teen girls in her care to visit the booth even though they were reluctant to be around police officers, whom they viewed with great disdain. (Children in residential treatment many times saw their parents arrested and/or were removed from parental custody by police officers, and as a result have learned to fear or even hate them.) Reluctantly, the girls went with Patty to the booth and were surprised by the friendly officers who were eager to share information about their animals and the joy they had gained through working with them. Patty watched the girls change from reserved and reluctant to happily interacting with the officers and their dogs. As they were about to leave, one of the officers stopped Patty and presented each of the girls with key chains, pictures of the dogs, and stickers. The girls smiled and thanked all the canine officers. Patty had the biggest smile of all, recognizing that the girls now had a changed view of the police. The reward of their time and sharing not only of gifts but also of information and even a laugh and a smile was priceless in showing the teens a new group of positive authority figures.

If you are able to keep in mind the principles set forth here, you will be well on your way to maintaining consistency in all that you do while on shift. It does, however, take work and practice to be consistent, and so do not let your guard down. Always remember the important nature of your work with children. Maintaining consistency should be a focus whenever you walk into your facility to begin your shift. Ask for help from coworkers and supervisors to gauge how well you are doing with your consistency and to learn ways to improve that are specific to you and your facility.

CHAPTER 9 REVIEW

1. Consistency means uniformity in all aspects of the job of a child-care worker.

2. Consistency allows children to feel safe and secure in the residential facility by offering certainty and assuredness in knowing that their environment will be the same from day to day–a departure from the chaos of their past living situations.

3. To maintain consistency you must strive to be the same and approach your work the same way every time you are on shift.

4. Childcare workers must enforce program structure and in all situations adhere to the program's policies and procedures.

5. The backbone of your program's structure–the house schedule–offers children a day-to-day assurance that they can count on you and your coworkers to care for their needs consistently. Not following the schedule is the quickest was to fail at consistency, but following the schedule is the easiest, most basic way to maintain consistency.

6. Maintaining good boundaries is critical to achieving consistency in your work. You must refrain from sharing personal informa-

tion with clients to keep the focus on them, where it should be. Do not try to be a friend; instead, be the positive authority figure they need. Acting outside of your scope of practice must be avoided. Be as fair and equal with each child as possible on every shift.

7. Setting limits is an important part of teaching appropriate behavior to the children in your care. Be sure that you are very familiar with the rules and consequences, but do not be afraid to look at them if you are unsure when an incident arises. Be sure to use the PWC method. Make sure to use "I" statements and treat the rules and consequences as a separate entity that dictates what you must do in order to take the personal aspect out of the interaction. Avoid power struggles and client manipulation.

8. Rewarding good behavior is equally as important as setting limits and in many instances is more effective. Be sure to reward children fairly and equally to maintain consistency. You must be very familiar with the reward systems in place at your facility. In addition, use praise liberally and consistently, making an effort to praise each child at least two times on every shift. Remember to key into each child's baseline behavior so you can reward according to the child's capabilities.

9. Role modeling appropriate behavior is a central aspect of your work as a milieu therapist. The children in your care will look to you to learn how to carry themselves, how to behave, and what it means to be a positive authority figure. Always arrive for work neatly dressed and well-groomed. Always maintain a positive demeanor while on shift. Maintain consistency by using good language skills at all times. Always be a role model of a positive authority figure by showing concern and caring for your client's needs, being able to make the hard decisions that adults must make when caring for children, following through whenever you tell a child you are going to do something, consistently rewarding client behavior to show that there is a positive side to adult authority figures, and showing fairness in your application of policies, procedures, rules, consequences, and rewards.

EXERCISES

Exercise One

Write down five things that you do on shift to maintain consistency.

1. _____

2. _____

3. _____

4. _____

5. _____

Exercise Two

Now write down five things that you can commit to do to improve your consistency.

1. _____

2. _____

3. _____

4. _____

5. _____

Exercise Three

In the space below, describe a time on shift when consistency was not followed. It could be an instance when you were the person who was not being consistent, or it could involve inconsistency on the part of a coworker.

Now describe the effect the inconsistency had on the children.

Finally, describe how the inconsistency and the problems it created were corrected and what, if any, consequences of the inconsistency were most difficult to handle.

Chapter 10

EFFECTIVE ON-SHIFT
VERBAL COMMUNICATION
FOR CHILDCARE WORKERS

Imagine a facility where little or no communication occurs among the staff. As an incoming staff member you would not know that five-year-old Danny has been having steadily worsening temper tantrums all day. You would not know that little Andrew has been complaining of a stomachache all day, his doctor was called just before you came on shift, and the doctor said that the boy should be taken to the emergency room if the pain persisted. Nor would you know that the facility social worker had been told by Bradley's county social worker to carefully chart his hygiene behaviors throughout the next month. You would not know that Ricky had assaulted a fellow childcare worker the day before, and that the childcare worker had to be taken to the emergency room for a broken wrist. As a result, Ricky had been placed on close watch, and childcare workers needed to be on alert to the possible need for a behavioral restraint should his behavior become out of control again. Without knowing these details, it would be very difficult to do your job effectively. You would constantly need to investigate what was happening and why as well as what special tasks had to be completed and why. Of course, all of this is not based on a real facility; indeed, it would be nearly impossible to imagine that such a facility with no communication ever existed. The scenario does point out, however, the vital importance of communication to good practice as a professional childcare worker.

The best way for professional childcare workers to maintain consistency both individually and as a group is through verbal communication among the staff. Verbal communication among staff on shift not only ensures that all staff are on the same page, but also keeps staff aware of what has occurred prior to their shift. Verbal communication will alert you to potential problems to look out for while you are on shift so that you can be prepared for what might occur. Knowing how important communication is makes it critical that you adopt certain procedures while on shift and to carefully comply with your facility's communication policies. You want to ensure that you and your co-workers are as well-prepared as possible for every shift.

While on shift you may also be called upon to communicate effectively with people outside of the facility. Verbal communication also includes interactions with parents, court-appointed special advocates, family, county workers, and other interested parties. It is important that you know how to respond and converse appropriately with the people that form the support for the children in your care.

VERBAL COMMUNICATION WITH COWORKERS

Preshift Update

When coming on shift, there is most likely quite a bit of recent history at the facility that you have missed. You probably have noticed that a lot has transpired if you were off for a few days and came back to work. Oftentimes, you may be surprised to learn of what has happened. You will need to know what occurred in detail. Of course, there will be time to glean historical information from written sources of communication as the shift progresses. However, you will need to have a semi-detailed overview when your shift begins. This kind of quick, yet thorough, updating can only come through verbally communicating with staff already on shift.

Although many facilities do not require it, good practice virtually demands that you have a preshift update before your shift begins. Always get to work ten to fifteen minutes before your shift begins and ask one of the childcare workers whose shift is ending to give you a rundown of what has been happening during his or her shift and since your last shift in as much detail as possible. Let your coworker know when you last worked so that he or she will know where to begin. Have a list of questions in your mind to pose if he or she does not cover them. You may want to write the list down on a small piece of paper and go down the list of questions so that you are sure you do not miss anything you need to know. That list could include the following:

Where there any special instructions left for my shift by the manager?

Oftentimes, the manager or supervisor will leave special instructions for tasks to be done on a particular shift. The list could include special instructions for a transport of one or more of your residents, what residents are eligible to attend a specific outing, or specific information to be given to a doctor when a resident goes for an appointment. Most times these instructions are left in a communication log or via notes or memos, but it will be most helpful for you to know about them before your shift starts by having outgoing staff point them out to you. This will save you the trouble of hunting for them and possibly missing some or all once the shift gets underway and the children are vying for your attention.

Is there anything I should be especially vigilant for?

Staff who have worked the previous shift are your best source of information about the "temperature" of the house before you arrived. Finding out what they have learned is so important for you to know as you start your shift. For example, outgoing staff can share with you their observation that two of the children were doing a lot of whispering and talking quietly to one another throughout the shift, which could portend that they are planning to go AWOL. You will be well-prepared to be especially watchful of them if you are given this information.

Is there a particular client who had a difficult time on your shift?

Outgoing staff will be in touch with any client who has had a tough time during their shift. Of course, the difficulties the child has had will not end when your shift begins, so you need to know the circumstances surrounding the child's problems that day and what interventions were tried, what interventions were unsuccessful, as well as what interventions appeared to help. This information will assist you in planning your interactions with any client who is having difficulty before your shift starts. You might even discuss what strategies the outgoing staff thinks might be useful to try and get feedback for ideas that you might have.

Could you give me a quick rundown of the
mood and behavior of each of our clients?

Getting a quick summary of each child's mood and behavior prepares you for what is to come when you hit the floor. You will be better prepared to address issues and "hit the ground running." Without this information, you would have to take the time to find out for yourself. With the information, you are ready to start working with the children right where they are emotionally, psychologically, and behaviorally.

Was anyone given consequences or special incident
reports within the last twenty-four hours?

Before you begin your shift you must know if any consequences were given for rule violations because this is perhaps the best indicator of the mood of the house or a particular client. When one child gets consequences, the mood and behavior of the children is often affected, either positively or negatively, and of course, the child who received the consequences may be experiencing a continuation of his or her negative behavior. Additionally, any special incident reports (SIRs) that were written would be most important to know about before your shift begins. An SIR is often an indicator not only that additional negative behavior is likely to follow but also that other children may become involved in the negative behavior. An SIR can also document an injury or serious illness, both of which you would need to be briefed on because you will be responsible for any continuing care.

Are there any new health concerns for any
of the children that staff are monitoring?

Children, especially those of latency age, are prone to colds and viruses. On any given day, when you arrive on shift there may be one or more children who are ill. You will need to know what medications were given to address the condition as well as what care was given to the child and what care needs to continue to be administered. Also important to know is whether the child has eaten or taken fluids on the previous shift.

Is anyone on safety watch? If so, what are the circumstances surrounding the safety watch?

Perhaps the most important thing to know upon arrival at work is who, if anyone, is on safety watch. Because there is a set of procedures to follow, awareness of the safety watch is critical so that you can immediately implement those procedures and network with other staff on shift with you to be sure that the procedures continue to be followed throughout your shift. You should also be informed of what led to the implementation of the safety watch so that you can be especially vigilant for triggers and behaviors that could indicate renewed distress on the part of the child on safety watch.

Have their been any behavioral restraints since my last shift?

You should also know if there have been any behavioral restraints used on the shift prior to yours. Ask the staff for the events that led up to the restraint and what the outcome of the use of the restraint was, for example, the child's mood and behavior improved. Be sure to ask if the child was appropriately counseled after the restraint was used.

Have any of the clients run away?

Particularly if you have not worked in a couple of days, you should ask if any of the children have run away since you were last at the facility. Let the staff member who is doing the briefing know the date of your last shift so that he or she understands what you know and do not know. If you do not know that a client went AWOL in your absence, you may have a moment of panic thinking that he or she has gone AWOL on your shift.

Have there been any instances of violence to self or others?

If a child is actively assaultive or self-harming, you should be aware of this when you begin your shift. You will need to work with other staff to plan interventions and ensure that the child is closely monitored at all times during your shift.

If you do not realize it already, you will soon recognize how important this briefing is when you come on shift. Most often you will have to "hit the ground running" right after your briefing, and the more information you have the better you will be able to approach your work. Later, when you have time to read charts and other written forms of communication, you will learn about what has been happening with each client in greater detail, but at the beginning of the shift the briefing is invaluable.

When called upon by coworkers who are starting their shifts to give them a preshift briefing, keep in mind the things that you want to know when starting your shift and impart that information to them. You may want to refer back to the list of questions you would ask during your preshift conference for further explanation of any of the points mentioned in what follows. Here is a list of some of the major things you will want to include when giving a coworker preshift briefing:

1. A summary of what occurred on your shift
2. A summary of what happened since your coworker's last shift— highlights only
3. Any special instructions that were left by supervisors for your coworker's shift
4. Description of any special concerns that you or your coworkers or supervisors have about any specific client
5. An outline of any change in behavior or mood from any specific client during your shift or since the last shift your coworker filled
6. A description of the mood of the house as a whole during your shift
7. Any instance of violence to self or others that occurred since your coworker's last shift
8. A quick rundown of consequences for rule violations that were given during your shift

9. Discussion of any clients who are on safety watch, the reasons for the safety watch, and if there are any special instructions attached to the safety watch
10. Ask the incoming staff if they have any questions once you have finished your briefing

Communicating via the preshift meeting will ensure not only that there is continuity from shift to shift, but also that staff are all working toward the same goals, watching for the same things, and taking appropriate steps to ensure client safety. The extra ten to fifteen minutes spent giving and receiving the preshift briefing will pay off for both clients and childcare workers.

On-Shift Communication

While you are on shift it is important that you and your coworkers are in communication at all times. Good on-shift communication ensures that the shift will run smoothly and consistently. Ineffective shift communication can lead to confusion, disorganization, and a lack of consistency. As we have seen, when consistency and order break down, children may begin to feel unsafe and acting out behaviors can occur. One of the most basic ways to keep a shift consistent is by communicating effectively with your coworkers. When staff are not communicating effectively, things can be overlooked. For example, dinner might not be started on time, the children are not ready to leave on time for appointments and activities, or important charting is left undone.

On shift, you and your coworkers function as a team. If the members of a football or basketball team do not practice good communication with one another, the team breaks down and becomes ineffective. The same is true with the team of childcare workers on every shift. Let us look at some ways you can make sure your team is communicating most effectively: location communication, consistency communication, delegation communication, and supervisor communication.

Location Communication

Location, location, location—true in real estate and also true on shift. At all times on every shift, you must know what your coworkers are doing and where they are. For example, if you are going to be involved with cooking dinner for the children, you should let your shiftmates know that you will be involved in the kitchen for at least fifteen minutes. This will allow the other childcare workers to plan their locations in the facility while you are engaged. Some facilities have yards or play areas where staff may take a child or group of children for a play activity. All staff should always inform other staff on duty when and whom they are taking into the yard for playtime. If you leave the house for any reason with one or more of your clients, you must tell your coworkers on shift that you are leaving, where you are going, and which clients you are taking with you. If you do not do this, staff may become concerned that one or more of the clients with you have gone AWOL. Here are some examples of how poor location communication can influence a shift.

Childcare worker John was scheduled to transport ten-year-old Travis to a dental appointment. As the two were getting ready to leave, another child, Kevin, started begging to go. John told Kevin that because the appointment would be brief he did not see any harm in his going along. Knowing that one shiftmate was busy with charting and the other was engaged in a craft activity with the rest of the children, John decided against informing them that Kevin would be going along on the dental appointment. A few minutes after they left, the childcare workers at the house noticed that Kevin was missing. They searched the house and grounds but could not find him. They tried calling John on his cell phone but it went straight to voice mail. Finally, just as they were about to call the police to report a missing child, John returned their call and told them that the child was with him.

Facilities for children can be rather large. One childcare worker joked that she could get lost inside her facility. When you add the grounds into the mix, you can easily see why the staff must be informed of each other's location if a crisis situation occurs. One such incident happened to Robin on one of her first days on the job at a girl's facility. Being new, Robin had a lot of questions, but she often had a difficult time locating the senior staff on duty because they were not communicating their locations effectively. Every time she had a question, Robin had to go searching for her coworkers to get the answer she needed. The children became frustrated with Robin who was frequently disappearing before returning with the information she needed to meet their needs. Robin quickly realized that the lack of good communication on shift threatened her relationships with the children, so she went the next day to speak to her supervisor. When Robin came in for her next shift, she found that her coworkers regularly communicated their locations to her, and things went much more smoothly. Her supervisor also assigned a childcare worker to work closely with her for her next couple of shifts to provide immediate information and guidance as Robin became more familiar with the facility.

Consistency Communication

Consistency communication keeps childcare workers on shift operating from the same script and on the same page at all times. Your shift will function like a well-oiled machine when you and your shiftmates have good consistency communication. As a result, the children will feel safe and well cared for, despite efforts they may make to divide staff.

Children in care are especially adept at "handling" childcare workers. Most have had a lot of practice and have come up with or been told some awfully smart ways of getting around the staff and getting around the rules. One of the most common methods is called staff splitting. Children want what they want when they want it. If an adult gives them the wrong answer to a request, they will seek out another adult and pose the same question, hoping for different results. Anyone who is a parent is well-familiar with this ruse. If Mom says no, time to ask Dad. If Dad says yes, contradicting Mom's response, the child is overjoyed, but problems begin for the parents, whose lack of communication not only caused inconsistency but also may cause friction between the parents.

In a residential setting, children regularly practice staff splitting or staff shopping, which involves asking the same question of as many staff as needed to finally get the desired result. For example, Maggie, a fifteen year old at Tyson's Group Home, wanted to prepare a batch of brownies about a half hour before dinner preparation was scheduled. She asked the senior staff, who told her to wait until after dinner, but Maggie was not ready to give up. She headed to the back of the house where she found a less-experienced staff member, who had no idea that the question was asked of the senior staff let alone her answer. Here Maggie got the answer she was looking for and went to the kitchen and started to make the brownies. Soon, Maggie's peer, who was scheduled to cook dinner, discovered the kitchen was a mess of flour, batter, bowls, and measuring cups. Unable to start dinner, Maggie's peer complained, and the staff became aware that they had been split. Fortunately, the consequences were minor—dinner was a little late and a few girls complained of being hungry. The senior staff talked to all staff on duty about the importance of communication while on shift.

When answering questions requiring permission that are posed by clients, it is often a good idea to check with other staff on duty to see if the question has already been asked and answered by another staff person. That way you can be sure that all of you are responding the same way to the question. Often you may not be aware of circumstances that would prohibit an affirmative answer to a child's query, whereas senior staff may have a more complete picture. When a child succeeds in splitting staff, there could be a serious break in program structure, so it pays to be especially vigilant and remain in constant contact with your peers.

"Staff splitting" becomes especially problematic for management personnel, whom the children see as having the right to override a childcare workers directive. Most managers have learned to check with the childcare workers before responding to a request or question. If a childcare worker has already said no, the manager must respond the same way. New manager Ilsa came to Robertson's Homes with relatively little experience but impressive academic credentials. During her first few weeks, she served as overseer of three of the company's facilities, spending part of her day at each one. After about a week of the children's getting to know her, Ilsa noticed that whenever she arrived at the next facility she found herself quickly surrounded by children, each with a question to ask her. "Can I take the ball out back and play," one asked. "Is it okay to stay up after bedtime tonight since we have a day off from school tomorrow?" another queried. "Can my friend Carla come over to visit tomorrow?" still another shouted while jumping up and down. Ilsa, seeing no obvious rule violations involved, said yes to each of the children, and then went to the staff office. By the end of her day at the facility, she noticed staff giving her the cold shoulder. After seeing this repeated at the other facilities, she finally asked the staff on duty what the problem was. Reluctantly, the childcare worker told Ilsa that the children were successfully splitting staff by asking Ilsa for things to which staff had already said no. Ilsa quickly learned that management staff need to be the most careful when it comes to staff splitting. From that day on she never answered a client's question without first going into the office and asking staff about the history of the request.

Childcare workers should have frequent verbal contacts with one another while on shift just to check in and make sure that all workers on shift are staying on the same page. Information of a confidential nature should be verbally shared in the staff office or somewhere that would not allow the other clients to hear. Especially in a large facility, staff should rotate staying in different parts of the physical plant to facilitate the informational check ins. For example, a childcare worker should not spend his entire shift outside in the yard with some of the children. Instead, every forty-five minutes or so another staff person should rotate to the yard. This will allow the two staff members to exchange information as needed during the rotation; at the same time, the staff member who had been in the yard can interact and share information with the staff who are inside the facility. These frequent verbal contacts among staff are essential to achieving consistency in communication.

Most facilities also have regular staff meetings that allow childcare workers to share information with other staff as well as supervisors. Staff meetings are invaluable tools in building consistency communication. Childcare workers can hear points of view and experiences of other childcare workers and get feedback from supervisors. Often during staff meetings treatment strategies will be discussed and planned, giving childcare workers a clear understanding of how to work with individual children. The communication that occurs during staff meetings helps childcare workers and supervisory staff maintain consistency through verbal communication.

Delegation Communication

The tasks required of staff on any given shift are many and can range from supervising children on a scheduled outing to completing entries in each client's chart. For a shift to run well, staff on duty must practice good delegation communication, meaning that they must be able to fairly and realistically divide tasks among themselves so that all staff on shift will understand exactly what specific tasks he or she is expected to do. Childcare workers on shift must communicate with regard to who will supervise activities the schedule requires for that shift. One childcare worker may volunteer to get the children ready on time and transport and accompany them on an outing. Another staff would then take care of supervising chores and dinner preparation, while another might handle the bedtime routine. This ensures consistency throughout the shift: the schedule will be followed, tasks will be completed, and the house will run smoothly. At some facilities, management staff may assign tasks to childcare workers for each shift. Other facilities elect to allow staff on duty to make those decisions, with senior staff taking the lead.

Meet briefly with your shiftmates at the beginning of each shift to discuss what tasks will be handled by whom. This meeting should not take more than five or ten minutes. Each staff person should know who will do what for the remainder of the shift. Keep in mind, however, that circumstances often change and the best-laid plans in residential treatment must be modified on a moment's notice. A crisis situation, a special incident, injury, or illness may arise on any given shift. Should this occur, you and your coworkers will need to regroup and redelegate tasks. The senior staff on duty should be in charge of assigning tasks, especially in a crisis situation.

Oftentimes, childcare workers will split the charting duties toward the end of the shift. By the end of the shift it has become apparent who has spent the most time with which client and would therefore be more capable of completing the charting for that client. Usually senior staff will talk with childcare workers on shift, and the decision will be made regarding charting duties. Staff will then need to decide how to rotate so the majority of staff are in the milieu while one staff person remains in the office to complete the charting.

At Aqua Home for Girls, childcare worker Marilyn enjoyed her job very much. One of the things she liked the most was knowing what her responsibilities would be whenever she arrived on shift. A self-confessed follower, she would have been uncomfortable with making shift planning decisions on her own, so she liked that senior staff were ready to brief her with what her major duties were for that day. Even in a crisis, Marilyn found that senior staff quickly told her what to do and where to be during the incident. Her experience was that things ran very smoothly even under tough conditions. Also, knowing what her major duties were for the shift allowed her some creativity within the framework of tasks. For example, on a particular shift she was responsible for the transport to a morning activity at the local gym, followed by supervising the girls at the gym along with senior staff. After returning to the facility, Marilyn was in charge of getting the girls lunch. Knowing there was downtime after that, she planned to play a game of Monopoly with any girls who wanted to join. Marilyn soon learned that moments like this were so important in building rapport and trust with the girls, and she took pride in her ability to come up with ideas to create opportunities for this to happen.

Supervisor Communication

Another way communication can ensure consistency is to conference regularly with your supervisors. Ask how you are doing at your job, and if there are any areas where you need improvement. If a supervisor is on shift, be sure to ask him or her what the priorities are for that shift and if there is anything special he or she would like you to do during your shift. If you have a question about anything, never hesitate to ask your supervisor. You will get the best information from your supervisor because of his or her wealth of experience in the field. If you want to learn more about your job, your children, and your facility in order to be better at your work and maintain consistency, there is no better source of information than your supervisors. Do not be nervous about approaching your supervisors. Most are more than happy to share their knowledge and expertise.

Senior staff on duty can also be a big help to you and are open to assisting you as you learn more about your work. Because these childcare workers are on shift with you, they are more accessible than management staff. They will have more opportunity to observe your work and give feedback, and they will also be more available to answer your questions and give you a deeper understanding of your job. Be sure to keep the lines of communication open, ask questions, and just simply pick their brains whenever you have the chance to do so.

CHAPTER 10 REVIEW

1. The most effective way to maintain consistency both individually and as a group is through verbal communication among staff.

2. When childcare workers arrive on shift, a verbal preshift update will bring them up to speed. They will be better prepared to face whatever challenges and responsibilities come their way.

3. Always arrive ten or fifteen minutes before your shift starts and ask one of the childcare workers whose shift is nearly over to give you a preshift update. Have a list of important questions memorized or carried with you to ensure that you get all the information you need. Be sure to tell the outgoing childcare worker when you last worked so he or she will know when to begin the shift history.

4. Good communication on shift is imperative if a shift is to run smoothly and provide the best care and service to children.

5. When you are the outgoing staff and are asked by incoming childcare workers for a preshift briefing, you should have in your mind a list of major topic areas you will want to cover with them to ensure that they are well-prepared for their shift.

6. Communicating via the preshift meeting ensures not only that there is continuity from shift to shift, but also that staff are all working toward the same goals, watching for the same things, and taking the appropriate steps to keep clients safe.

7. While on shift, good communication with other childcare workers is essential. Childcare workers on shift function as a team, and a team cannot act effectively if there is poor communication.

8. Be sure to communicate your location to other childcare workers and know where your shiftmates are at all times. This is especially important when leaving the facility with one or more children. You must make other staff on shift aware that you are going and which children are going with you.

9. Consistency communication keeps childcare workers on shift operating from the same script and on the same page at all times.

10. Consistency communication will prevent manipulations such as staff splitting.

11. Childcare workers should have frequent verbal contacts with one another while on shift just to check in and make sure that all workers on shift are staying consistent.

12. Regular staff meetings allow childcare workers to share information with other staff as well as supervisors and are invaluable tools in building consistency communication. Often during these meetings, treatment strategies are discussed and planned, giving childcare workers a clear understanding of how to work with individual clients.

13. Delegation communication, which refers to fairly and realistically dividing all of the tasks that occur on a given shift, assists staff with making sure all the duties and responsibilities of the shift are taken care of.

14. Childcare workers can maintain consistency in their verbal communication by seeking regular conference with their supervisors. Senior staff on duty are also good sources of helpful input and information.

EXERCISES

Exercise One

Describe how your facility handles the assignment of tasks for each shift.

Exercise Two

Jot down five question about your work that you would like to ask your supervisors or senior staff on duty.

1. _____

2. _____

3. _____

4. _____

5. _____

The next time you have the opportunity be sure to ask these questions!

Chapter 11

EFFECTIVE WRITTEN COMMUNICATION SKILLS FOR CHILDCARE WORKERS

Another way to remain consistent in your work as well as to maintain consistency among childcare workers, management, social work staff, and mental health professionals is via written communication. Most facilities will have a variety of ways that the staff regularly communicates with each other from shift to shift, such as individual client charts, staff communication logs, and SIRs. Written communication fills an important function in keeping staff operating as a team and following the same treatment plans and strategies with the children in their care.

Childcare workers and managers must be informed of what occurred with each client on every shift during which they were not present. Written communication in the form of charts, logs, and other documents provides a record of what has happened with each child on each shift day after day. When a client does anything remarkable either positive or negative, it is recorded in some fashion in one of the many written forms of communication at your facility. This record can be referenced and used to track client progress, plan treatment interventions and strategies, and assess client needs.

Written communication provides reference of what childcare workers need to know about events that occurred since their last shift as well as the day they are working, Although the preshift verbal briefing gives the incoming staff a quick summary of what has been happening since their last shift, written communication, such as individual client charts and communication logs, offers a more complete and detailed picture that will allow staff to more fully understand the dynamics that have occurred in their absence.

All of the written communication that you complete at your facility is a therapeutic record of each child's behaviors and functioning that
can be accessed by social work staff, county caseworkers, and mental
health staff (a record that can be subpoenaed in a court proceeding).
A review of a particular child's daily chart can be used to track behavior and mood and can assist a county caseworker in making decisions
related to the appropriateness of that child's placement. A mental health
worker, such as a psychiatrist, may refer to charts and logs to help him
make decisions about medications. Your program social worker especially values all of the charting that you do because it is an essential
part of her job to review the information and share pertinent details
with members of that child's treatment team that may include her
county caseworker, court-appointed special advocate, family, and
mentors among others. The program social worker also relies on your
written communication on each child to formulate treatment plans
and strategies. Written communication on each client is also essential
when the program social worker is writing her quarterly and discharge
reports.

Many staff are uncomfortable with the writing aspects of their work,
but childcare workers quickly recognize the importance of keeping
good written records. It becomes clear to them the first time a childcare worker relies on a written record to plan her shift or to understand a particular client's mood or behavior. Childcare workers, management staff, and mental health professionals appreciate good written
communication. It makes everyone's job a lot easier and their work
more professional. Without written communication to reference while
on shift, childcare workers would have to function with little or no
background information on their clients. Whereas verbal communication can give a quick rundown, written communication goes deeper,
offering details and instructions that may be missing from verbal brief-
ings.

THE THREE MOST IMPORTANT ELEMENTS OF A WRITING TASK: SUBJECT, AUDIENCE, AND PURPOSE

Every writing task is written on a particular *subject* for a specific
audience to accomplish a specific purpose. Understanding each of these
three aspects will help you to focus on detail that needs to be includ-

ed, eliminate detail that does not need to be included, have an understanding of the kind of tone and word choice to use, and direct your writing to be most effective and appropriate. Decisions about content, tone, and direction will be made so much easier if you are able to incorporate consideration of the subject, audience, and purpose into any writing task that you are given on the job. Here is an example of how consideration of subject, audience, and purpose influence a writing task. Let us say that you were going to write a letter to your grandmother (audience) telling her about your new boyfriend (subject). Your purpose would most likely be to let your grandmother know what is going on in your life and to reassure her that you are making wise choices. You would most likely include details about your boyfriend's employment, family, and character. Now let us change just one element of the writing task—the audience. For this letter you are writing to your best girlfriend. Can you see how this would change the letter completely? Your purpose, of course, would be quite different as a result of the audience change. When writing to your best friend, you would most likely be trying to "toot your own horn" at least a bit and impress her with your good fortune. The content of the letter would change dramatically, with an emphasis a bit more on looks and less on character.

Writing is not easy. Any writing task requires a myriad of decisions on content, tone, or word choice, just to name a few. Speaking is spontaneous and comes naturally to almost everyone. If you miss a detail or your listener does not understand what you have said, he or she can ask a question for clarification. There is a give and take that helps the speaker focus on what the listener needs to know about, and what details are important to the listener. Not so with writing. You do not get the chance to have that give and take that will assist you in making content and other decisions about your subject matter. Most childcare workers find verbal communication with coworkers to be much preferable to a writing task that will be shared with their coworkers. In fact, most childcare workers say they find writing tasks to be the most difficult single responsibility of their jobs.

The good news is that there is help. The information presented in this section will be of assistance to your future writing on the job. If you employ the specific suggestions and considerations detailed here, your writing will improve. The exercises at the end of the chapter will also help further illustrate important points and give you practice at employing new techniques. Like just about anything, practice helps. The more you write, the better you will become, especially if you make use of the techniques you will discover in this chapter. Maybe you will not learn to love writing tasks on the job but you will likely find them easier and more bearable.

Audience in Your Writing Task

Your audience for any writing task consists of the primary people who will be reading what you have written. Much like writing a letter to a specific person, as we have seen, the audience for your writing task directs you to choose the details, tone, and words that will be most appropriate for them as they read what you have written. For example, you would not use the same tone and language in an SIR that you would use in a note on a daily chart. The audiences are vastly different. An SIR is written for an audience of county workers, court-appointed special advocates, and licensing analysts. In an SIR your tone must be professional, without the use of slang or words that convey your personal feelings or emotions. Slang has no place in an SIR unless you are quoting someone involved in the incident. The note on the daily chart is a different story. Here you are writing directly to your client. You need to include a tone that is appropriate for the situation. For example, you can express disappointment if the child has broken a rule or his or her behavior was inappropriate on your shift. On the other hand, you can lavish praise if a child's behavior was good on your shift. If you see a child who needs your encouragement, you will want to offer a positive message that will help her or him become motivated. You can use a much more common vernacular here and not be so formal. The writing in the daily chart note should be much more conversational, as though you were actually talking to your clients. In fact, if you wrote to your clients the same way you wrote to a county worker in an SIR, you would likely encounter a less than positive reaction from your clients when they read what you have written. Your clients might find you to be distant and uncaring about their situation. The opportunity to motivate them and teach them about their behavior would be lost. Likewise, if you used the same language and tone in an SIR that you used in a note on a daily chart, your audience would find your communication to be unprofessional and not helpful in communicating the events of the SIR.

Any writing task may also have one or more secondary audiences— readers for whom the writing is not directly targeted but who will also read the document. The most common secondary audience is other childcare workers, who will likely read the document as part of their review of what occurred since their last shift or when filling out a child's behavioral chart. Other secondary audiences will most likely include your program social worker, program manager, executive director, and members of your company's board of directors. It is important to note that secondary audiences rarely have as much impact on the composition of a specific writing task, but they are worth mentioning to give you the scope of influence of your writing and a clear idea of the people who may read it.

Whenever approaching a writing task, you must consider who will be reading what you are writing. This consideration of audience will allow you to decide which details need to be included and which do not. You will also be able to make decisions about word choice, tone, and level of formality. Know your audience before beginning any writing task.

Purpose in Your Writing Task

The purpose in your writing task is the reason that you are writing and what the written word is meant to accomplish. Having a clear sense of purpose as you write will assist you in deciding what needs to be included and what does not. Purpose will also help you determine your tone, vernacular, and word choice. Let us look again at the two very different tasks of writing an SIR and a note on a child's daily chart. Your purpose in writing an SIR is to inform your audience of what occurred during an unusual event that affected one or more of the children in your care. You will want to provide enough factual detail so that your reader can "see" what happened as well as what staff did to respond to the situation. When writing a note on a child's daily chart, your purpose is to provide the child with appropriate feedback on his or her behavior during your shift. In any given note, your purpose may be to offer praise or encouragement or to express disappointment as you give the child your observations.

Consideration of purpose defines the writing task that you might tackle. Knowing that you have a reason for writing helps you to understand the task at hand. Relating to those reasons will give you a clearer picture of what your writing needs to accomplish for your reader(s).

Subject in Your Writing Task

The subject of any writing task you do on the job is the thing, person, or event about which you are writing. If you are writing shift notes in a child's chart, your subject is that child, what he did, how he behaved, and how his moods manifested during your shift. When writing a note to your coworkers about a safety watch procedure that is in effect, your subject would be the details of the procedure and how they relate to the children in your care. When you are writing an SIR, the details of the event, what staff did to respond to the event, and how the incident was resolved are the subject. The subject is what you are writing about, but inherent in some writing tasks are certain subject elements that are required for the goal of the writing task to be accomplished. For example, an entry in a child's daily chart should include mention of the activities in which she participated, notations on her mood and behavior, detail of any consequences that she received during your shift, and any rewards that were given. An SIR must always include a fact-based accounting of the incident, how staff intervened in the incident, and what things staff did to respond to the incident, as well as what follow-up will be done.

HELPFUL HINTS

Most childcare workers possess writing skills that are sufficient to provide good written communication to other staff. If you are self-conscious about your writing skills, as many people are, here are some good rules to follow:

1. Stick to the facts.
2. Use the journalistic questions plus one.
3. Move in chronological order.
4. Do not inflate your language.

Following these basic guidelines will help you improve your written communication and raise your confidence level about your writing.

STICK TO THE FACTS

When writing on the job, you must stick to the facts. Include only what you have observed or heard. If you did not see it, it did not happen. You can include what was reported by someone else, but you must say that it was reported and by whom. Here is an example of how this might work. Let us say that you and another childcare worker were supervising a group of children when a boy named Tom kicked a boy named Jenson, which started a physical altercation between the two boys. After you and your coworker dealt with the incident, you were asked to write an SIR. The writing problem is that you did not see Tom kick Jenson, but, fortunately, your coworker did. In your report you should write

> *Childcare worker Smith (your coworker) said she observed Tom kick Jenson, which started the physical fight between the two . . .*

In this way you are accurately portraying the incident and sticking to the facts while including the observations of your coworkers. If your licensing representative has questions about the incident after reading the report, he or she will know to whom to address any follow-up questions regarding the events.

Sticking to the facts also means that you do not give your personal opinion, editorialize, or use words that tend to convey emotion or judgment. Again, this means only writing about what you have seen or heard or what a coworker has seen or heard by report. Avoid using descriptors like adjectives or adverbs. Also avoid words that imply that you have made a conclusion or judgment about the facts. Here are some examples of failing to stick to the facts and how to improve.

Too Many Descriptors

Childcare worker Glen tried *valiantly* to separate the two boys, but Eric, the *imposing* older of the two, kept *furiously* swinging.

Marcus, *a slightly built youngster,* tried to escape. CCW Glen blocked Eric's path, allowing the *whimpering* Marcus to escape.

Just The Facts Revision

Childcare worker Glen tried to separate the two boys, but Eric, the older of the two, kept swinging. Marcus tried to escape. CCW Glen blocked Eric's path, allowing Marcus to escape.

Notice how eliminating the italicized words, which are the adjectives and adverbs, does not detract from the account. Instead, removing the descriptors gives a more professional fact-based telling of the events. Let us look at another example that involves making conclusions or judgments about the facts.

Making Conclusions or Judgments About the Facts

Evelyn *had been acting crazy* all day. At seven in the evening, she *stormed* into the kitchen and *went over the edge,* throwing apples at her peers.

Conclusions and Judgments Revision

Throughout the day Evelyn appeared to be talking to herself and laughing and crying without provocation that staff could observe. At seven in the evening, she went into the kitchen and began throwing apples at her peers.

In the first sentence of the example, the writer makes a conclusion about Evelyn's behavior instead of showing what her behavior was. In the revised version, clear examples of what the writer observed Evelyn doing paint a better picture of the day than the conclusion-drawing words do. The word "stormed" editorializes and makes an emotional judgment. Better simply to state the fact that she went into the kitchen. The phrase "went over the edge" not only lacks a professional tone but also once again makes a judgment about Evelyn's behavior. In the revised version, the actions that were observed by the writer speak for themselves.

Use the Journalistic Questions Plus One

Because most of the of writing you will do involves an accounting of what occurred on your shift, it is important to go with what happened and stick to the facts. News writers make use of the journalistic questions to make sure all the facts are covered in a writing task. Childcare workers should also use the journalistic questions for the same reason, but for our purposes we must add a question that particularly applies to the writing done by childcare workers:

1. Who is it about?
2. What happened?
3. Where did it take place?
4. When did it take place?
5. Why did it happen?
6. How did it happen?
7. What did staff do to respond? (the plus one question)

Using these questions will keep you focused on exactly what happened. Let us look at an example.

One Friday evening, a fourteen-year-old boy named Justin, gets into a verbal altercation with another boy named Carlos. Both boys are sitting in the television area watching television when Carlos changes the channel while Justin is watching his favorite program. Soon the two boys are yelling at each other. Childcare worker Bart and another staff member, Matthew, intervene and attempt to separate the two boys by asking Carlos to come into another room to talk to Bart while Matthew asks Justin to sit down on the sofa and talk. Before Carlos leaves the room he throws the remote at Justin, just missing his head. Bart manages to get Carlos to leave the room while Justin stays with Matthew.

Now let us apply the journalistic questions to this example:

Who is it about?

It is about clients Justin and Carlos and childcare workers Bart and Matthew. (Notice that the childcare workers who were present during the incident are included.)

What happened?

It was a verbal altercation between Justin and Carlos and the throwing of the remote by Carlos at Justin. (When answering this question, you must get to the heart of exactly what occurred by summarizing it in a single sentence or two.)

Where did it take place?

It took place at the facility in the television room. (Be sure to include the larger location [the facility in this case] as well as the more specific places within the larger location, in this instance the television room.)

When did it happen?

It happened on Friday, April 21, 2008, at 8:35 p.m. during a scheduled television viewing period. The "when" of the incident encompasses not only the date and time but also what was taking place according to the house schedule.

Why did it happen?

It occurred because the two boys became upset over the changing of a television program. (Here you would write your assessment of what led to the incident.)

The Plus One Question

To properly complete most writing tasks as childcare workers an additional question must be added to the journalistic questions: what did staff do? Your audience will be focused on how the staff responded and intervened when any special incident occurred, but they will also be looking for how staff interacted with the children in your care throughout your shift. County workers, licensing analysts, and special advocates will be especially interested in how staff interacted with residents and what they did to respond in crisis situations. Your supervisor will also be very interested in what you did to handle any situation that arises on the job. It is important to consider this question separately to ensure that its answer is adequately represented in your writing. Let us take a look at how this question would be answered using the preceding example.

What did staff do to respond to the situation?

Childcare workers Bart and Matthew responded to the situation and separated the two clients. The childcare workers processed with the clients individually, and both clients calmed down and returned to the milieu. While processing, Carlos decided he needed to apologize to Justin, and CCW Matthew accompanied Carlos when Carlos apologized to Justin. The two clients shook hands and returned to the milieu.

Notice how much detail is included in the answer to the plus one question: What did staff do to respond? You will need to write out what you did to take care of a situation to satisfy requirements by licensing, caseworkers, and your supervisors. When you are writing about a special incident, you must include how you and fellow staff intervened, how you resolved the situation, and how you returned the house to normal, following the schedule and reintegrating involved clients into the milieu.

Move in Chronological Order

One of the most difficult aspects of a writing task is organization. Inexperienced writers often get bogged down in the details and have difficulty organizing the facts. The result is that readers have a difficult time following and may not understand what occurred during the incident you are attempting to document. Organizing based on chronology offers the easiest way to stay on track as you detail any incident. Chronological order also helps the reader follow the events in a natural, realistic manner. In the writing you do as a childcare worker, the key is having your reader—whether it is a county worker or a fellow childcare worker—readily understand any incident you must describe. Keep in mind that the use of chronological order provides a solid basic framework for any writing task that you face.

The easiest way to organize most of your written documentation is to use chronological order. Start from the beginning; for example, the beginning of your shift or the beginning of the incident is a good place to start and move to the end. As you move in chronological order, be selective of what facts need to be included in order to understand what happened on your shift or during an incident. If you include every detail, a report or entry could grow into a treatise. Choose only those facts that are important for the reader to know. Take a step back from the writing task and then tackle it, asking yourself, "Would I need to know this fact in order to understand what happened?"

Do Not Inflate Your Language

Many inexperienced writers make the mistake of believing they need to inflate their language or use big words in order for their writing to be considered good. Quite the opposite is true. For writing to be good, it must be clear and get its point across to the reader. If your reader is sent running to the dictionary for every other word because you used a thesaurus to inflate every other word, your point will not be made effectively. Indeed, considering what makes good writing, some of the worst writing is that which uses inflated language. Avoid using a thesaurus whenever you are writing at work. Only use words that you know and understand. Those are the words that your readers will be most likely to easily comprehend.

MOST COMMON WRITING TASKS
FOR CHILDCARE WORKERS

The Staff Communication Log

Most facilities have some sort of staff log that communicates to incoming staff in writing what has happened during any given shift—positive and negative. The staff log should contain a brief outline of the events of the shift, taking care to highlight any unusual incidents or incidents that may be of concern. Often the staff log is used to alert staff that clients may have been acting out or received consequences for their actions during the shift. The log also points out if any residents are on safety watch, which will let incoming staff know that they need to keep a close eye on the clients and restrict their access to sharps. Managers appreciate feedback on planned outings to let them know if clients did not like the outing or refused to attend, which will help them in planning future activities. Some facilities use a narrative format in which the events of the shift are written out in a paragraph or two; others use a format in which each client's initials are written and two or three lines are provided for shorthand significant facts about each on that shift. Either way, the purpose of the staff log is to provide information about the previous shift to incoming staff so that they can be prepared for their own shifts.

Here is an example of how a portion of a good staff log shift entry might go:

Ct. A: *Woke up, did hygiene, attended activity, and enjoyed herself; positive behavior*

Ct. B: *Had trouble waking up on time, did not complete hygiene, refused activity, had verbal altercation w/staff; irritable mood, received restriction*

As you can see, just the highlights of the shift are included to give incoming staff a quick overview of what happened before they go on shift.

Client Charting

An ongoing client chart containing progress notes is a common feature of most residential programs for children. The progress notes need to be completed once during each shift by the childcare workers who were on duty during that shift. In the progress notes, childcare workers provide more detail on the client's behavior, activities, and actions on that shift than was provided in the staff log. In this way, the body of the progress notes becomes a record of each client during his or her stay at your facility. In the progress notes a narrative accounting must be given. When writing the progress notes, you want to highlight the important things that happened with that child during your shift, including good points and bad points. When a person has finished reading a shift entry he or she should have a good idea of that client's behavior, actions, and attitudes during that shift.

Because the progress notes assist incoming staff in their understanding of each client's mood and behavior on the previous shift, you can set a framework for what detail needs to be included by asking yourself the question, "If I were coming on shift, what would I want and need to know?" Include only those details that answer that question. Use a chronological format to organize the details you include. If an incident occurred on shift, use the journalistic questions plus one (what did the staff do to respond?) to decide what details need to be included.

Remember that the social work staff and mental health staff at your facility will read what you have written as a reference to discover how the client is doing. In addition, the court may subpoena progress notes. Keep your entries professional in tone and word choice. Do not use slang expressions or inject your own feelings. Here again, the facts are called for. To deviate from the facts is not a professional representation of yourself or your facility, and it renders the progress notes less useful to all. If you have opinions or suggestions regarding anything that happened on your shift, it is better to talk to your supervisor rather than writing it down in the progress notes.

Let us look at an example of a good progress notes entry:

> *2/15/07 9:10 PM   Client had a positive evening. Client completed his homework and did not complain about having to do it as much as usual. After eating a good dinner, client offered to help staff pick up the toys that were scattered in the family room. Client showed good initiative and follow-through. Client had some difficulty falling asleep and complained to staff that he couldn't sleep. Staff encouraged him to return to his bed. One staff suggested he count sheep. Client had not heard of this and thought it was a funny idea. Staff told him to visualize little sheep jumping over a fence and count them as they came over. Client said he would try it. When staff did the next bed check fifteen minutes later, client was fast asleep. C. Smith, Childcare Worker*

Notice how the example covers the significant events of the shift and gives an idea of the client's mood and behavior throughout. You will also notice the repeated use of the word "client." It is a good idea in your most of your writing at work to avoid using pronouns as much as possible. In some of the writing you will do on shift, pronouns can and usually do become confusing. For example, if you work at an all-boys facility and you are writing about an incident that involved three of the boys, after a few uses of the pronouns "he," "him," and "his," it may become difficult to tell to which of the nouns (the boys' names) the pronoun refers, making it hard to tell who did what to whom.

Progress notes are generally written at the end of the shift because the narratives must reflect the entire shift. It is important to plan ahead in your mind and set aside time at the end of the shift to write in client charts. If you do not, you may write a hurried entry that does not do a good job of communicating what occurred during your shift. Also, only one entry need appear in a client's chart per shift, so you and your coworkers can share the load, with each taking an equal number of clients to write about so that no one has to do all of the writing in all of the progress notes for that shift.

Special Incident Reports

In most jurisdictions, residential facilities for children are required to document "special incidents." A special incident can be defined as any incident involving a client that is unusual and serious in nature, such as an injury, being AWOL, hospitalization, suicide attempt or ideation, alleged child abuse, physical violence, the use of a behavioral restraint, police involvement, or property destruction. The purpose of the SIR is to provide information about the incident to county caseworkers and state licensing analysts, keeping them informed of what is happening with a particular child as well as how you and your coworkers are handling issues dealing with the children's health, safety, and well-being. SIRs can be subpoenaed in court proceedings and are likely to be read by a number of important people outside of your facility who are involved in a given child's life. In addition, SIRs provide your coworkers, social work and mental health staff, and supervisors with valuable information regarding what exactly happened in often very serious situations that can arise. The SIR helps staff know what to expect when they come on shift. For example, if an SIR from earlier that day indicates that a child had out-of-control behavior that resulted in his needing to be restrained and placed on safety watch, incoming staff will know not only to keep a close eye on that child but why they need to do so.

When writing an SIR, it is important to stick to the facts. County caseworkers and licensing analysts sometimes received forty or fifty SIRs a day and do not have the time to wade through your personal opinions and observations. They want to know the facts of what oc - curred without editorializing. Remember to use the journalistic questions plus one. The plus one question–"What did staff do to respond?"–is of the utmost importance in an SIR. Licensing analysts and county caseworkers are especially interested in what staff did to assist with the situation and bring it to a conclusion. Since the SIR is a business record and as such a legal document, what is contained in the SIR represents the official record of what happened during the incident. If you and your coworker did ten different things to respond to a given incident, but you did not write them in the SIR, it will appear that you and your coworker did nothing to intercede in the incident. As a state licensing analyst once told me, "If it isn't written down, it didn't happen." Imagine that you were called to give testimony in court about the incident and were asked, what happened? If you talk about what the client did and the events as they happened but do not mention what you did to help, the judge and/or jury will have all the facts. They cannot consider what they have not heard. You cannot go back after your testimony is over and ask for a do over. So it is with an SIR, if you do not put it in at first you cannot add it later. In fact, anything added later will lack the same credibility as the original.

When you write an SIR, licensing workers read it to make sure that your facility is responding appropriately and that licensing regulations are being followed. Licensing analysts also look to make sure that your facility is maintaining a safe environment for the children and watch out for possible safety hazards, for example, play equipment that is broken and caused an injury to a child, as well as how well staff is endeavoring to intervene and protect all the children. A county caseworker generally reads incident reports with the same critical eye, looking for similar things as licensing analysts, but they are also concerned with the specific child and his or her specific case. The county caseworker will be trying to ascertain if the child is correctly placed; for example, does he need a higher level of structure and supervision. The caseworker may also want to discuss the child's program with your facility's social worker and psychologist or psychiatrist to determine if a change in the treatment plan is needed or if outside services need to be added. Overall, the SIR is added to the child's permanent file by the caseworker, where it will form a part of the record of the child's behavior and actions that will be used when the caseworker has to make her regular written reports to the court whether the child is a probation or dependency placement. In the case of mental health placements, the SIR may provide information that the caseworker will want to include in a scheduled or emergency meeting called an individualized education program (IEP) to discuss school placement or allocation of services to the child.

Client Behavioral Systems

Many facilities have behavioral programs for the children, such as daily charts or level systems, that require staff to write short notes to each child acknowledging both positive and negative behavior. If your facility has such a writing task, it is important to note that you will need to make a complete change of tone, purpose, and content, because you are now writing to the client. Of course, supervisors will read what you have written and it must be appropriate, but the audience, unlike other writing tasks, is not colleagues or professionals who work with your facility and the children placed there. Instead, the readers are the children with whom you work. Your goal for the short notations you write on behavioral program forms is to encourage the child when she does a good job. Entries like "Way to go! Great job cleaning your room!" or "I was so impressed by how polite you were when we were at the restaurant. You were so nice to the waitress, and your table manners were awesome. Good for you!" are good entries that reward children with praise when they do well. On the other hand, notations must be made when a child does not perform well or breaks a rule. In these instances, it is better to be somewhat encouraging, to offer to help, or to express disappointment. Actually a combination of all of these may be the best strategy whenever possible: "Manny, I was so disappointed that you didn't make your bed after I asked you to do so. I know you can do better than that. Maybe next time I can help you get started, and you'll see it will be done and looking great in no time."

If your facility has behavioral charting of any kind that the children are able to see, you will quickly notice that the children are very interested in what staff have written and will ask to see their charts (if they are not posted in the milieu) and will read them carefully. The children are most interested in the feedback they get from staff. Of course they relish the positive feedback, but they also read the comments on negative behavior as well and will in some way, big or small, sooner or later, begin to incorporate the suggestions into their behavior. This kind of direct written communication with your clients is so important and critical in bringing to fruition their treatment goals. As with writing in progress notes, this writing is generally completed at or near the conclusion of your shift, because you need to draw upon the behavior throughout the entire shift. For example, a client's mood and behavior may have changed dramatically from the beginning to the end of your shift, and notations written at the beginning of the shift may be inaccurate. At the end of the shift, childcare workers may be understandably tired and anxious for their shift to be at an end so they can go home and relax. Sometimes staff will write out notations on behavioral charts in a hurried or even careless fashion because they are already dreaming of being off shift. Considering how important to clients the behavioral charts are it is critical that you plan your shift to set aside time at the end to carefully and conscientiously write on the children's behavioral charts, taking full advantage the therapeutic value the charts have for your clients. Because in most cases only one entry needs to be made per shift, you can split up the charts with your coworkers, each taking the clients with whom they had the most contact during the shift. This lightens the load and makes it easier to focus on the task at hand.

Staff Memo

Another form of written communication you will encounter is the staff memo. Oftentimes, supervisors will write periodic memos to staff when problem areas are identified. A memo might be written to explain a particular procedure that the staff are having repeated questions about or a memo might be written to explain a rule change that staff do not understand. Sometimes memos are written to point out areas where staff need to be more conscientious. For example, overnight staff may not be completing required filing tasks, or the evening shift may be leaving the kitchen a mess. In this case the memo may be a step taken before disciplinary action to give staff a chance to correct missteps before things become more serious. Memos are also frequently written to introduce new rules, policies, and procedures to staff. Usually this type of memo contains a lot of detail and answers any questions staff may have. In all cases, memos are important for communication between management and staff and most often contain information critical to your job performance. As a childcare worker, you must carefully read and study any and all memos that come from your supervisors. If you have questions after reading a memo, do not hesitate to see your supervisor and ask for more information.

CHAPTER 11 REVIEW

1. Written communication provides reference for what childcare workers need to know about events that occurred since their last shift as well as the day they are working.

2. All of the written communication completed at your facility is a therapeutic record of each child's behaviors and functioning that can be accessed by social work staff, county caseworkers, and mental health staff. It forms a record that can be subpoenaed for a court hearing.

3. The three most important elements of any writing task are a consideration of subject, audience, and purpose unique to that particular task.

4. Audience in a writing task consists of the primary people who will be reading what you have written. Much like writing a letter to a specific person, the audience for your writing task directs you to choose the details, tone, and word choice that will be most appropriate for them.

5. Purpose in your writing task is the reason that you are writing and what the writing is meant to accomplish. Having a clear sense of purpose will assist you in deciding what needs to be included and what does not.

6. The subject of any writing task is the thing, person, or event about which you are writing.

7. When writing on the job, you should stick to the facts. Include only what you have observed or heard or been given by verbal report from another childcare worker or in some instances a client. You should avoid giving a personal opinion or observation, unless it is specifically requested.

8. Use the journalistic questions plus one: who, what, where, when, why, and what the staff did to respond.

9. You should always move in chronological order, which provides an easy way to organize your task and also the clearest approach to your content.

10. Do not feel the need to inflate your language. Your vocabulary is generally fine. There is no need to run for a thesaurus.

11. One of the most common writing tasks for childcare workers is the staff communication log, a place where staff provide brief summaries of each client's behavior and activities during shift.

12. Client charting is perhaps the most important among the common writing tasks a childcare worker must tackle. The chart entries form a record of a child's behavior, activities, and actions while he or she is at your facility.

13. SIRs are required to document "unusual" occurrences, such as clients going AWOL, suicide attempts, client injury, and so on.

14. The writing that staff does on client behavioral system is quite important because it provides feedback to clients about their behaviors and responsibilities and where they stand in the program.

15. The staff memo is an important means of communicating significant information to childcare workers as the need arises.

EXERCISES

Exercise One: Subject, Audience, and Purpose

In the lines below, write three of the most common writing tasks you tackle in on the job.

1. _____

2. _____

3. _____

Now for each of the tasks identify the subject, audience, and purpose. Then write about how the consideration of these basic elements of a writing task will change the way you approach each task.

Task 1:_____

Subject:

Audience:

Purpose:

My new perspective on the task:

Task 2:_____

Subject:

Audience:

Purpose:

My new perspective on the task:

Task 3:_____

Subject:

Audience:

Purpose:

My new perspective on the task:

Exercise Two: The Journalistic Questions Plus One

Using an incident that you can recall from your work, apply the journalistic question plus one. For confidentiality's sake, change the names of all those involved.

Who (include staff and residents):

What (events that occurred during the incident):

Where:

When (include more than just the time of day but also include what scheduled things were occurring):

How (how events unfolded):

Why (the reason[s] behind the incident):

What staff did to respond:

Exercise Three: Writing About an Incident

Using the incident to which you applied the journalistic questions plus one, identify your subject, audience, and purpose as applied to that incident.

Subject:

Audience:

Purpose:

Now, using the information that you have acquired examining subject, audience, and purpose and answering the journalistic questions plus one, write about the incident as though you were completing an SIR. Do not forget to use chronological order to help organize the information.

Chapter 12

KNOW YOUR MILIEU

As a childcare worker, much was explained about the physical aspects of the milieu when you underwent your initial training. You learned where things were stored and were probably surprised by the amount of things kept throughout the facility. At some point you were shown a key ring containing many different keys that fit all the locked items in the facility. Your trainer explained that licensing regulations require that certain things be kept under lock and key, and by the end of your training you were expected to know which lock belonged to which keys. Most likely, you got a rundown of which client was assigned to which room, where the recreation areas were located, and in which room the children generally congregated. You also needed to learn about the laundry facilities and where the laundry products were stored. In the kitchen, there was a lot to know: where the plates, the flatware, the drinking cups, and the pots and pans were. Likewise, in the office, there were many locked boxes, binders for different logs and charts, and equipment such as the fax machine, phone system, printer/copier, and computers. The outdoor areas were also explored, and you learned where the trash cans were located, what areas were safe for the children to play, and where to park your car when arriving for work. Of course, this is just a sampling of all that you were required to learn during your initial training, and when you add to that learning all of the rules and consequences, reward systems, protocols, and procedures and simply getting to know your clients and coworkers, the whole initial training experience can be quite overwhelming. In the midst of all the information you must process, sometimes the milieu itself gets lost. You and your trainer may overlook the physical aspects of the milieu, and you may forget to utilize what is there or simply de-emphasize its importance as everything else swirls around in your head.

The milieu of your facility can be your best resource and most important asset and a critical player in an emergency. It is the place where you spend the most time with the children in your care, and the children can have fun and just be kids. With your assistance and knowledge of the milieu, children can have a positive experience as you utilize the resources your facility has to offer them. A game of Monopoly can help two children who were having a conflict begin to feel more comfortable with each other. When children are bored, your milieu has a lot to offer–a DVD of a current movie that you can all watch together with a bowl of popcorn, a dip in the swimming pool, or playing on the jungle gym in the backyard. With a little imagination and creativity combined with a thorough knowledge of your milieu, each day can offer fun, positive experiences and learning opportunities. On the other hand, the milieu is also where most of the children's acting out behavior occurs. Here again, knowing your milieu can assist you in effectively dealing with the negative and even dangerous behaviors your clients may display. Your knowledge of the milieu can help you better manage these types of incidents along with your facility's policies and protocols.

This chapter takes the physical plant aspects of the milieu and looks at the milieu in a different way, as both a resource and a support for your job as a childcare worker. Forming the backdrop for your work and the home for your clients, the milieu represents security and safety for your clients and, as a result, a place they can be children and work and play knowing they are protected. As a childcare worker, utilizing your milieu to its fullest potential can enhance the day-to-day experiences for the children in your facility. First, however, you must know your milieu and what it has to offer and how it can ensure the safety of the children in your care.

FLOOR PLAN AND LAYOUT

Take some time when next on shift and carefully familiarize yourself with the layout of your facility. Note where all of the clients' rooms are and which child is in each room. Look at the areas for storage as well as where items for general usage are kept, noticing all closets.

Walk through the bathrooms and laundry area. Stroll the common areas, including television room, living room, dining room, and recreation room. Make a special tour of the kitchen to remind yourself where items are stored, including condiments, spices, utensils, pots, bakeware, measuring cups and spoons, and pitchers. Take a look in the garage and familiarize yourself with items stored there. Walk around the staff office and take notice of storage and maintenance of things constantly used by staff, including medication storage and log; client charts; staff communication log; client behavioral charts; and phone, fax, and computer resources, to name a few.

Because the milieu contains so many different and important elements, it may be a good idea to complete a walk through the facility every month or so to keep things fresh in your mind. Knowing the layout of the milieu, including where things are stored and kept, will assist you in more quickly and efficiently meeting your clients' needs. For example, if a child asks you for a Q-tip® and you have no idea where they are, you could take a long time searching for one. As we discussed, meeting client needs in a timely manner is important to role modeling a positive authority figure. Sometimes clients may require that you be able to respond to requests quickly under certain situations. If a client is ill and vomiting in the bathroom, has used up all the toilet paper in the room, and is asking for more, you must be able to respond with a new roll as soon as possible. When the kitchen timer has rung and the cake in the oven is done, if your client cannot find any potholders and asks staff for help–fast or it will burn–you must know where to find what she needs without hesitation.

Your walk-through of the milieu should be done with an eye to places where children can hide. Experienced staff know that when a child cannot be found and suspected of going AWOL, the child is often eventually located hiding somewhere in the facility or on the grounds close to the house. Some common places children can hide in the milieu are in a bedroom closet, in an unlocked storage or coat closet, behind and under furniture, in bushes or behind vegetation, and in alleyways or around the side or back of the house. Familiarizing yourself with potential hiding spots allow you to better respond and intervene when a child is under emotional stress and agitation and return him or her to a safe environment where you and other staff can assist him or her in processing the problem at hand.

About once a month, you should try to walk the outside of the facility, including the back and front yard areas. Look for potential hazards, such as holes in the ground, protruding rocks, or low-hanging branches. Report any hazards you notice to your supervisor as soon as possible. Take note of places where children could hide on the outside of the facility. If you have playground equipment, make sure that you know where and what it is, and it does not hurt to check for potential hazards there, such as broken or loose parts. Once again, let your supervisor know if you find any hazards.

Knowing the floor plan or physical plant of your facility is the first step in truly becoming aware of what the entire milieu has to offer. Being regularly in contact with all areas of the milieu will also keep you aware of potential problems that you can report to your supervisor. Above all, your regularly familiarity with these aspects of the milieu will make you better able to respond quickly and efficiently during a special incident.

SAFETY FEATURES

In your initial training you were no doubt shown all of the safety features and plans that your facility has in place. However, this information came when your brain was filled with the mountain of information you were learning about your new facility and possibly, if it was your first job in the field, your new career. Topics such as which emergency exits to use in the event of an emergency may have gotten lost in the overflow of detail and data. Unfortunately, also, many of us do not focus on safety issues as carefully as we should—even though we know we should. I can prove my point by asking a simple question, "When did you last change the batteries in your smoke detector?" If you answered the last time I set the clocks back for daylight savings time, you are probably in the minority.

Although you may focus on safety more in your own home, on the job as a childcare worker, the safety features of the facility may take a back seat because you are dealing with meeting client needs, handling client problems and disputes, calming acting out behaviors, and simply tackling the many tasks required on each shift, such as charting, assisting in the administration of medications, and making sure the schedule is being followed. On shift there is a lot to do and a lot to remember. Children are constantly approaching you with needs and requests. The phone is ringing and you must leave a written message for the program manager or social worker. The children are asking to use the phone or arguing over which television program to watch. Another child is refusing to do his homework–again. Because of the hectic and demanding nature of your work it is important that you know and remember your facility's safety features and how to use them.

In order accomplish this, review the safety features and procedures on a biweekly basis. Because you will need to act in a split second should a safety emergency occur, being very familiar with what to do is of the utmost importance. Not only will you have to respond, but also you will have to oversee the response of the children and the staff and do so in a calm orderly fashion without a hint of upset or panic. If you do not have your facility's safety responses engrained in your brain, you may not be able to succeed in protecting the children and role modeling the way a positive authority figure handles a crisis.

Most facilities are required to post emergency evacuation plans. Every two weeks you should carefully review this plan. Walk the routes that children will be instructed to travel to evacuate the house. Notice which of the children's bedrooms are closest to each exit. Keep a constant eye out for anything that obstructs any of the emergency exit routes and immediately move it. In addition, most facilities are required to have regular fire drills for residents. Make sure that you are well-familiar with the fire evacuation plan, including the location where everyone is instructed to meet up after leaving the facility. In an emergency there is no time to look up what you and the children are supposed to do in the event an evacuation is needed. You must already know it and know it well.

State regulations require that residential facilities for children have working fire extinguishers located in areas of the house that are prone to flash fire, such as the kitchen and the laundry room. Know where the extinguishers are in your facility and periodically verify that they have remained in the same location. If they have moved, ask your supervisor about the new location. Oftentimes, extinguishers are inadvertently moved when an area is cleaned, but its location may be stipulated as a specific place. If this is so, your supervisor would want to know if the extinguisher has been moved so he or she can return it to the proper location.

If you ever need to use the extinguisher, knowing how to operate it is of vital importance. Many facilities provide the extinguishers but fail to inform staff about their use. Here are some basics about when it is not appropriate to use a fire extinguisher:

1. Do not use the extinguisher if you do not know what is burning. The chemicals in the extinguisher could interact with the burning substance and cause an explosion or toxic fumes could be created. If you do not know what is burning, call the fire department (911) immediately.
2. If you have a rapidly spreading fire, the time to fight it yourself has passed, and you need to call 911 immediately.
3. You should not try to use an extinguisher if the fire appears to be too large to be knocked down by the extinguisher you have.
4. Do not try to use the extinguisher if your instincts tell you not to do so. Better to call 911 and allow professional firefighters to do the job.

If you decide it is appropriate to use a fire extinguisher, make sure that you are between the fire and an unblocked exit, so that you can get out if you need to. A clear exit should always be at your back. Using the fire extinguisher is not difficult if you can remember the acronym PASS. Follow these basic steps:

1. *P*ull the pin: Pulling the open allows discharge of the extinguisher.
2. *A*im at the base of the fire: Do not aim at the flames; instead aim at the bottom, where whatever is fueling the fire is located.
3. *S*queeze the handle or lever: This will release the extinguishing agent.
4. *S*weep from side to side: Do this until the fire is out completely. Start the sweeping motion from a safe distance away and then as the flames go down move in closer. After you have the fire out, keep an eye on it for hot spots in case the fire reignites.

Using a fire extinguisher is easy if you keep these simple rules and suggestions in mind. It is a good idea to regularly review fire extinguisher procedures so that you can automatically spring into action in case of a fire emergency.

Sharps are another area of safety concern in residential facilities for children. Most states require that sharps be locked up and only dispensed when they are to be used and then immediately returned to the locked box or drawer when the child has finished using them. Your facility should have at least one lock box or drawer for keeping sharp items out of common circulation. In homes for small children, for the most part it will be staff that use sharps such as kitchen knives, screwdrivers and nonchild safety scissors, but these staff must take care not to leave these items lying around in the milieu where children could pick them up and injure themselves. The potential slip most likely to happen is when a staff person uses a paring knife to prepare food, washes it, puts it in the dish drainer, and leaves it there. Staff must take care to immediately dry off the knife and return it right away to the locked container. A sharp knife should never be left in the dish drainer. In facilities with older children who help with the cooking as part of an independent living skills program, childcare workers must supervise the use of a sharp knife at all times and ensure it is immediately washed and locked up when the client is finished using it. Children should never be allowed to handle kitchen knives unsupervised. In homes that work with teenagers, shaving razors become an area of safety concern. Razors should be signed out and immediately returned after using. Children should never be allowed to keep a razor after it has been used.

We have covered only a few of the safety features that residential facilities for children employ. Most likely there are many more safety precautions, plans, and procedures that you were introduced to during your initial training. It is a good idea to occasionally review all of the safety features that your facility employs. If you have any questions or would like to know more about any of them, ask your supervisor. He or she will be happy to explain the safety features in more detail. After all, in residential facilities for children, safety is and should be a primary concern for all childcare workers.

TRANSPORTATION VEHICLES

The vehicles in which you and your coworkers transport your clients to and from activities, outings, and appointments are likely to be large multipassenger vans. Some may require drivers to hold special licenses in order to drive them because of their size and passenger loads. However, most of the vehicles used in residential care will not require a special license; they will often be large, unwieldy vehicles to drive. Most residential facilities will offer behind the wheel training in their fleet of vans before you are allowed to transport passengers. Because of their size, these vans can be tricky to maneuver, especially around parking lots and on narrow streets. Even pulling into a driveway can be tricky for someone who has no experience driving a larger vehicle.

If you are not completely comfortable driving a large vehicle, take advantage of whatever behind the wheel training is offered at your facility. Do not be embarrassed to request additional training if you feel you need it. Your supervisors would much prefer that you feel comfortable and safe when transporting clients. Be sure to become very familiar with all of the features of the vehicle, such as windshield wiper switches, headlight controls, heating and cooling system regulators, and so on. When you are making your first trips in the vehicle, take a few moments to review the important features of the vehicle before driving, and, of course, do not forget to adjust your mirrors.

Many insurance companies that specialize in the residential care industry offer safe driver training courses for free or a minimal cost. Your facility may already be offering such a class. The material included in these classes provides a review of some safety aspects but also adds new and important information for all drivers. Even seasoned drivers who have been safe behind the wheel for more than twenty years have found they have learned more than a few things from taking safe driving courses. Most of these programs offer a certificate upon completion. You can never be too safe behind the wheel, especially when carrying your special cargo—the children in your care.

RESOURCES

When you first toured the facility where you work, you no doubt noticed the home contained a wealth of resources for the children to play with, create with, and enjoy. Unfortunately, many times little time is spent familiarizing you with the many resources that are available for your use and the children's use. This information probably got lost amid the mountain of detail you needed to learn to begin to do your job effectively. The truth is that these resources, such as toys, games, arts and crafts supplies, and sports and playground equipment, can be some of your most important assets when working with the children in your care. Take some time on your next shift and check out all of these resources that are there for you and the children to enjoy.

Books can be a great way to communicate and interact with children, especially younger ones. A book can be a great icebreaker if a child seems depressed or unsure of you when you are new to a facility. Offering to read a youngster a story and letting him choose the book almost always has positive results. The child's mood will brighten and he will feel more comfortable interacting with you. Of course, books are educational and you can use the opportunity to test and challenge a child's reading and vocabulary skills. Books also stimulate a child's imagination and creativity. You can even invent games and activities around the book you have just read together. For example, you might have the child draw a picture of one of the characters or tell his own story about what might have happened where the book left off.

Children of all ages love card and board games. Teenagers may complain as teens do, but once they get involved they will have fun, sometimes in spite of themselves. Playing games together builds camaraderie among the group, improving peer relations as well as client to staff relationships. Become familiar with the games that your facility has to offer. Take some time to read up on the rules of the ones you do not know and the ones you might not have played for a long time. Ask the children which games they like and locate them. Whenever there is a lull and children seem bored or low in spirits, pull out one of those games and get them playing. Most likely you will see things change. Children enjoy playing games for prizes, too. Some facilities offer game night challenges, where small prizes are offered for winners. If your facility does not do this, you might want to suggest this to your supervisor.

Arts and crafts are another way to engage children in activity. From coloring to making bookmarks to more complicated hobbies such as knitting and crocheting, children enjoy creating. They are very proud of their finished pieces and relish the praise they receive. Make sure that you know what arts and crafts supplies are available at your facility so you will be ready to use them when you need them. For example, if you see a child sitting alone while the other children are watching a video, you might want to ask her if she would like to color with you in one of the coloring books in the playroom. You can then quickly access the coloring books and crayons you need. You will find that doing arts and crafts together builds rapport with the child and often can get a child to open up to an adult. Psychologists do not specialize in art therapy for nothing. It is a proven method of successfully working with children and some adults.

Outdoor equipment, such as sporting goods and playground features, encourage children to exercise and get fresh air. Studies have begun to show that children do not get enough physical exercise. In addition, exercise can be an excellent stress reliever and can truly help emotionally disturbed children feel better about themselves. If your facility has a yard, you can engage the children in many team games, such as baseball, kickball, and soccer. Team sports encourage good peer relations and a healthy spirit of competition. Your facility may also have such equipment as swings or sliding boards. Utilizing these resources with children can have benefits.

CHAPTER 12 REVIEW

1. Your milieu can be your best resource and most important asset, as well as a critical player in an emergency situation.

2. Know the floor plan of your facility well so that you can respond to client needs and are familiar with resources that can be used to engage and entertain the children. Doing a regular survey of the milieu will keep you up to date on new resources and will also help you identify potential hazards that need to be reported to your supervisor, such as long hanging branches or tripping hazards both inside and outside of the facility.

3. Be familiar with your facility's safety features and review them every two weeks.

4. Be very familiar with your facility's emergency evacuation plan.

5. Regularly review the locations of house fire extinguishers and know when and how to use them. Know the PASS method–the correct way to use a fire extinguisher.

6. Understand and follow to the letter your facility's procedures for sharps.

7. Take advantage of on-the-job training in driving techniques for facility vehicles, which often are large vans that many staff have little or no experience driving. Do not be afraid to ask for additional training if you feel you need it.

8. Take time to check out all the resources that your facility has to amuse and entertain the children, such as games, DVDs, craft activities, and sports and playground equipment. You never know when a strategically placed invitation to play a board game or shoot a few hoops will be invaluable in de-escalating a child and keeping order at the facility.

EXERCISES

Exercise One: Safety Features

On the lines below write five specific safety features at your facility.

1. _____

2. _____

3. _____

4. _____

5. _____

Exercise Two: Emergency Exits

Next, write down the location of two exits that can be used in an emergency evacuation.

    1. _____

    2. _____

Exercise Three: Facility Resources

Write down seven specific resources at your facility that you have used or could use to entertain the children.

    1. _____

    2. _____

    3. _____

    4. _____

    5. _____

    6. _____

    7. _____

Chapter 13

TAKING CARE OF YOU

The profession of a childcare worker can be very stressful. As we have seen, the children in your care come from troubled backgrounds and continue to manifest behavioral, emotional, and psychological problems. While on shift, you may have to deal with tantrums, out of control behavior, and emotional outbursts and, in some facilities, may have to place a child in a behavioral restraint to protect her or others. At the end of some shifts your dealings with clients may leave you feeling tired and emotionally and physically drained. You may just want to crawl into bed with a cup of tea at the end of a particularly difficult shift.

Many in the helping professions are so focused on caring for others that they forget to care for themselves. Because childcare workers are generally giving people, they often lead lives that are focused on giving to others and neglect their own well-being. In their article, O'Halloran and Linton (2000) point out that

> The challenge lies in the fact that wellness is a concept that we as counselors often focus on more readily for our clients than ourselves. Counselors who are trained to care for others often overlook the need for personal self-care and do not apply to themselves the techniques prescribed for their clients. (p. 354)

Ironically, giving childcare workers may offer solid advice on how to deal with stress, depression, and heightened emotions to their clients, but then they do not follow their own advice and take care of themselves and use the same advice in their personal life. When childcare workers do not care for themselves, they risk health problems, relationship difficulties, and burnout. Health problems can arise as stress builds. Workers may not be getting enough sleep, or sleep may be interrupted by periods of wakefulness or disturbing dreams that may be related to work. Stress may cause childcare workers to overeat to comfort themselves or to suffer from a low appetite. Any or all of these health effects of stress can lead to a multitude of health difficulties if the childcare workers do not attend to the underlying issues of job stress. Some childcare workers may experience difficulties in their personal relationships as stress builds and causes them to become ill-tempered or withdrawn. Unfortunately, those closest to them will be affected most by the stress-related behavioral changes in their loved one.

Burnout is a common danger for everyone who works in a helping profession. Dealing day in and day out with difficult clients can take its toll. It is not uncommon for childcare workers to experience burnout, which describes a state of mental, emotional, and/or physical exhaustion. Once burnout has set in, childcare workers are no longer able to do their job effectively. They simply do not have the wherewithal to perform to the level of their abilities. When supervisors recognize that a childcare worker is experiencing burnout, they will insist that the worker take at least one week's vacation from the job. A good supervisor will also recommend some of the healthy living practices described in this chapter.

Margo was a childcare worker with years of experience in the field. Her work was always highly praised in performance reviews. Most of her work in the past had been part-time, but she had recently been promoted to full-time work. One night after handling a crisis situation with a client, Margo went home and could not sleep. She tossed and turned and continued to gaze at the alarm clock. She did not follow any of the advice she gave her clients when they could not sleep—reading a book, drinking warm milk or chamomile tea, or listening to a relaxation tape. She kept running over and over the events of earlier that evening in her mind. Soon it was time to get out of bed and get her children off to school. She had gotten no sleep that night. The same thing occurred the following night, although she did manage an hour or two of sleep. Later that evening while on shift, she made errors on two of the children's medication sheets and dozed off while watching television with the boys. Fortunately, her coworker nudged her awake. Margo felt horrible.

Alice, another childcare worker, worked part-time at a group home for boys. She loved her work, but she had a hard time dealing with the stress of the work. Alice found that when she left a shift she worried about the boys and their problems. She rolled over and over in her head events that occurred on shift and fretted over whether she had handled things correctly. It did not seem to matter to her that her performance reviews had been good since she started her job. One day her supervisor noticed she had dark circles under her eyes and looked very tired. The supervisor asked Alice if she was taking care of herself. Alice recounted to her supervisor what had been happening. Alice could only laugh to herself when she heard the advice her supervisor gave her; it was the same advice Alice regularly gave to her clients, but she had completely forgotten to apply it to her own life.

It is vitally important for you to take care of yourself to stay on top of your game so you can provide the best service to your clients and to avoid burnout. Although many of the suggestions and techniques we have discussed in previous chapters will help you avoid burnout and keep you fresh and focused on shift, stress can still be a factor simply because of the nature of your work. All childcare workers should carefully consider their own physical, mental, and emotional health and well-being and make feeling healthy a priority for both themselves and their loved ones as well as the deserving clients with whom they work. Your clients deserve the best "you" possible. You must keep yourself healthy in order to be there for them and do your job to the best of your ability. Let us look at some suggestions for self-care that will help keep you healthier and limit your stress level.

DO NOT BRING YOUR JOB HOME WITH YOU

Just as you leave your personal issues at the door when you enter your facility, you must leave your work at the door when you leave. Taking your job home with you can create stress in your personal life. If you are dreaming about your clients, thinking about things that happened on shift while you are enjoying an evening with family or friends, or are unable to sleep because you are concerned about a particular client, you are taking the baggage of your work home with you. The result can be increased stress level, difficulty sleeping, fatigue, and loss of appetite or overeating. You may also experience difficulties with your relationships with friends and family because stress causes you to become short tempered or distant.

Make a conscious effort as you exit your facility to deliberately leave your work at the door. Many childcare workers find that a simple visualization helps. Imagine that you are putting all of the events of the shift–your day's work–into a suitcase. As you leave the facility, visualize that you are putting the suitcase right outside the front door where it will remain until you report for your next shift. You might try imagining as you exit the facility that the stressors of your shift drop slowly from your body as you walk to your car.

Robert, a childcare worker at a home for young boys, spent a lot of his free time researching on the web. He looked up the psychiatric diagnoses his clients suffered from, or he searched new and interesting activities for the boys he could suggest to his supervisor. He also read books written by and about children who had been in residential treatment. Because Robert lived alone, he could spend a good deal of his time focusing on his work. He worried about the children who were having troubles maintaining in the facility. He wondered what would happen to them if they had to move to a higher level of care. Soon Robert began to have dreams about his job, and in those dreams Robert always did something wrong–he did not follow procedure, he forgot to check on boys who were on safety watch, or he failed to complete paperwork that was required of him. One day a coworker noticed that Robert looked troubled and asked what was wrong. The coworker was able to gently tell him that he was burning out because he was too focused on his job in his off time. She suggested visualization, and Robert began to put it into practice. It took some time, but after a while Robert learned that for his own good and that of his clients he needed to leave his work at work.

If you find that you are consistently bringing your work home with you, talk to your supervisor. She or he will be able to offer additional suggestions and counsel.

MAINTAIN PERSONAL RELATIONSHIPS

It is important that you have a strong support system of friends and family in your life. Spending time with your family and friends provides an excellent way to escape from the pressures and stress of your job as a childcare worker. Having a strong and nurturing personal life is the key to living a happier, healthier life. Many experts believe overall happiness is measured by the quality of relationships in a person's life.

In Robert's case, while he was bringing his job home with him, he focused almost exclusively on work and neglected his relationships with his friends and family. Friends would call and suggest activities, but Robert was always too busy or too distracted by work to accept their offers. Robert's mother became concerned because her son rarely called her. When she called his brother and sisters, they also said they had not heard from him much in recent months.

After Robert began, at his coworker's suggestion, to use the "leave the job at the door" visualization, he started to realize that he had neglected his personal relationships. He soon began to reconnect with friends and socialize with them, and he started calling his mother and siblings several times a week as he had in the past. Also, he made sure that a couple of times a month he spent time with his niece and nephew. He always had a wonderful time when he took them to amusement parks or just out to an arcade. The change back to his old self made Robert feel much better about himself, and in turn, he found he was much more effective at his work.

While not on shift, take time to focus on the relationships in your life and strengthen and nurture them. As you focus on the support people in your life, the stress of your work will diminish. Like Robert, you will feel better about yourself and will be much more effective as a childcare worker.

LIVE A HEALTHY LIFESTYLE

Keeping yourself healthy means that you will be mentally, emotionally, and physically ready for the challenges of the profession of childcare worker. Eat a healthy diet. Limit your intake of sugar, fats, and salt. Try to eat the recommended amount of fruits and vegetables every day. You will feel better and you will be ready for anything on the job.

Childcare workers should have a regular exercise routine. Not only does exercise help relieve stress; it also keeps your body healthy and strong. Try working out at a local gym or YMCA, take a yoga class, try Pilates, or simply take a brisk walk several times a week. Be sure that you check with your doctor before you start exercising, especially if you have not previously incorporated exercise into your lifestyle.

Some people find that enriching themselves spiritually is a big part of a healthy lifestyle. Attending a religious institution on a regular basis can assist in staying relaxed, centered, and focused and can add to one's overall health. Many people find that regular meditation or relaxation exercises are very helpful in relieving stress and keeping mentally and physically fit.

Margo had difficulty sleeping because she had trouble managing the stress of her work with children. When she began to apply the advice and counsel she regularly gave her clients to herself, Margo added exercise to her daily routine. She started off with brisk walks on the advice of her doctor, and then later she joined a gym and worked out on the equipment three days a week and took a yoga class whenever she could fit it into her schedule. After a few months Margo never had a problem sleeping, and she felt so much better physically. In addition, she felt like her mind was clearer than it had been in a long time. In all facets of her life, including her job as a childcare worker, Margo became more productive and more confident.

ENJOY RECREATIONAL ACTIVITIES AND HOBBIES

In order to stay healthy and reduce stress, every childcare worker should have an active and satisfying personal life outside of his or her job. Recreational activities and hobbies such as swimming, fishing, hiking, sewing, cooking, or writing help you escape the demands of your work and focus on you. Childcare worker Carol finds that knitting afghans for friends and family is an excellent stress reducer, and she gets the pleasure of presenting her creations to those she cares about. David enjoys playing guitar and singing at local coffee houses.

As you focus on your hobby or activity, the stress of your work will seem far away.

If you do not have a hobby or recreational activity in which you regularly participate, find a quiet moment and sit down and make a list of the things you enjoy doing and things you would like to do but never took the time. Most of you will find that you can come up with quite a list. Put the list away for a day or two and then return to it. Make a choice of your top three items and make a plan to accomplish one or all of them. If you need to attend a seminar or find some instruction, check out resources in your community.

Carol, childcare worker at a facility for teenaged girls, was experiencing job stress after three of her clients went AWOL and did not return to the facility. For her, it was the first time in her short career she had experienced the loss of a client, and to have three go at once was especially troublesome for her. Her supervisor suggested that she practice some relaxation techniques and maybe consider taking a few days off. Almost in a joking manner, he told Carol, "Why don't you try getting a hobby?" Carol laughed, but something sounded right about his suggestion. She began to try to come up with ideas of hobbies she could try out. Soon she realized that she had always wanted to learn how to knit. Since she liked to work with her hands, Carol thought it might be perfect. She had no idea how to knit but she knew her grandmother could teach her. After a couple of hours of instruction from her grandmother and some practice, Carol has become skilled with knitting needles. She now happily donates her handmade blankets to residents at a local nursing home. Above all, Carol finds that when she is knitting it is like her stress just melts away. Her boss's silly suggestion turned out to be an important part of her life.

David, like Carol, was having difficulty managing the stress created by his job. A coworker shared with him that he had taken up a hobby, and it had been a big help to him in dealing with the stresses of his job. David had always dreamed of playing guitar and writing songs. He decided to try to pursue his dream in the hope that it might help him better handle the stress of his job. He already had an acoustic guitar and knew some rudimentary chords but realized he needed help. After finding a teacher, he began to practice hard and found he really enjoyed playing. Soon he was writing songs and, after some encouragement from his friends and his teacher, he started playing at small venues near his home. David experiences much pleasure and satisfaction from his hobby, and he has little time to focus on the stress of his job.

PERSONAL COUNSELING

Many working in the counseling field find that therapy helps them deal with the stress of their work. A good therapist can suggest ways to cope effectively and reduce your stress level. You can learn to improve your coping skills and more effectively handle work pressures. Seeing a therapist is a good idea, especially if you find your work is creeping into your personal life and relationships or if you are having difficulty sleeping, have increased anxiety, or are suffering from poor appetite or are overeating. Also, many childcare workers and those in the helping professions in general find that their work may trigger some deeper issues that had been buried or were thought to have been resolved. Should these kinds of issues arise, it may become difficult to function personally and professionally. A therapist can help you work out these issues and improve your overall mental health and well-being.

Alice, whose constant worry about the children at the group home where she worked was interfering with her lifestyle and her health, decided that seeing a therapist was something she would like to try. During her first session Alice told the therapist about her work and how she was not managing the stress very well. Within a few sessions, Carol had learned some strategies for better coping with the stressors in her life, which included her job. She enjoyed her sessions with the therapist and found that she learned a lot about herself that would benefit her not just on the job but in all areas of her life.

In addition to the stress that comes with the territory of milieu therapy, you may find that working with children will trigger reactions and behavior that may surprise you. Things that happened to you in your own childhood may come up as you deal with your clients. Your own issues of abandonment, sibling rivalry, abuse, codependence, or need to rescue can emerge and affect you and how you do your job. If you are experiencing problems coping at work and in your personal life, a therapist can assist you in working through your personal issues. You will begin to feel better, and your job performance will improve.

A childcare worker new to the field, Serena found that she grew very attached to one of the young girls with whom she worked. Serena would bring special little presents for this girl, whose name was Crystal, and secretly give them to her. One day while on shift she whispered to the child that she would take her out for ice cream. She went into the office and took the keys to the house van. Her co-worker Amanda asked her what she was doing. "There's nothing on the schedule," Amanda told her. "Oh, I know," Serena replied, "but I just thought that I would take Crystal for some ice cream since she's been so good today." "Whoa, wait a minute," Amanda said. "What about the other girls? They have been good too." Serena made her way toward the door and called for Crystal. "Well, I'm just going to take Crystal. I think she deserves it the most." Serena then quickly exited the house with Crystal. Amanda was perplexed. She had not seen Serena go against policy before.

Unfortunately, Amanda realized she had no choice but to inform Serena's supervisor. The next time Serena came to work she was called into her supervisor's office. Serena was very worried that she was going to lose her job, so she was very honest with her supervisor when he questioned her about Amanda's report. Although she did not think anything was wrong with it, Serena told her boss that she had become attached to Crystal. The supervisor recognized right away that Serena was developing a rescue fantasy, and he counseled her on the subject. Serena soon understood that she was on a course that could be harmful to her and to Crystal. Her supervisor suggested that she might try going to some sessions with a therapist to try to understand how she developed the rescue fantasy, especially if she wanted to continue working in the field.

Serena took his advice and was able to learn a lot about herself and what motivated her to attempt to connect so deeply with one of her clients. It took about six months of therapy before her therapist felt that Serena had successfully come to understand her tendency toward a rescue fantasy and to put in place coping skills to assist her in dealing with this tendency. Although Serena admitted the therapy was sometimes difficult, she did feel that she benefited greatly from the treatment. She continued her job as a childcare worker, a career she loved, and she never crossed the boundary into a rescue fantasy again.

Ask family, friends, and associates or your doctor for referrals if you would like to see a therapist. Talk to the therapist either in person or over the phone before committing to work with him to make sure that you feel comfortable with him and his approach to therapy. It is often a good idea to talk to more than one therapist before making your choice. In most communities, there is an abundance of therapists from which to choose. If you cannot get a referral and have to choose from the phone book, the interviewing process is especially important. Most insurance will cover some or all of the cost of therapy, but if finances are an issue, many clinics offer counseling on a sliding scale.

CHAPTER 13 REVIEW

1. The job of a professional childcare worker is a stressful one that attracts caring and giving people who in their desire to assist others frequently neglect to care for themselves.

2. It is vitally important that childcare workers care for themselves so that they can provide the best service for their clients.

3. Childcare workers who fail to care for themselves may experience burnout—a mental/physical/emotional breakdown of sorts—that prevents them from functioning optimally in all areas of their lives, including on the job.

4. One way of avoiding burnout is to refrain from bringing your job home with you. Just as you leave your personal issues at the door when you enter the facility, you must leave your work at the door when you leave. If you dream about your clients or cannot sleep because you are concerned about a client, you are taking your work home with you. In this equation there is little room for relaxation and escape from job stress that your body needs to recharge itself.

5. Another way of caring for yourself is to maintain your personal relationships and have a strong support systems of friends and family. Spending time with your friends and family will help you

to relax and enjoy your life and escape from the stress of your work.

6. Living a healthy lifestyle is an important way to maintain your readiness for your job—mentally, emotionally, and physically. For many childcare workers a regular exercise routine is important. Others may rely on a strong sense of spiritual health and nurturing through attendance at church.

7. In order to stay healthy and reduce stress, every childcare worker should have an active and satisfying personal life outside of his or her job that includes a variety of recreational activities and hobbies.

8. Many who work in the counseling field find that therapy helps them to deal with the stress of their work. Childcare workers might consider engaging in a course of therapy to assist them in dealing with the stressors of their work and the personal issues their work may trigger.

EXERCISE

Without looking back at the list you made in Chapter 1, make a list of what you think are the ten most important qualities or characteristics of a good professional childcare worker.

1. _____

2. _____

3. _____

4. _____

5. _____

6. _____

7. _____

8. _____

9. _____

10. _____

Now compare your two lists. How are they different and why?

BIBLIOGRAPHY

Anglin, J., Denholm, C. J., Ferguson, R. V., & Pence, A. R. (Eds.). (1990). *Perspectives in professional child and youth care.* Binghamton, NY: Haworth Press, Inc.

Appelstein, C. D. (1998). *No such thing as a bad kid: Understanding and responding to the challenging behavior of troubled children and youth.* Weston, MA: Gifford School.

Bleiberg, E. (2001). *Treating personality disorders in children and adolescents: A relational approach.* New York: The Guilford Press.

Crone, J. E. (1984). *Getting started as a residential childcare worker: A guide for beginners.* Washington, DC: Child Welfare League of America, Inc.

Durkin, R. (1990). Competency, relevance, and empowerment: A case for the restructuring of children's programs. In J. Anglin, C. J. Denholm, R. V. Ferguson, & A. R. Pence (Eds.), *Perspectives in professional child and youth care* (pp. 105–118). Binghamton, NY: Haworth Press.

Durrant, M. (1993). *Residential treatment: A cooperative, competency-based approach to therapy and program design.* New York: W. W. Norton and Company.

Fewster, G. (1990). Growing together: The personal relationship in child and youth care. In J. Anglin, C. J. Denholm, R. V. Ferguson, & A. R. Pence (Eds.), *Perspectives in professional child and youth care* (pp. 25–40). Binghamton, NY: Haworth Press.

France, K. (1993). *Basic psychological skills for front-line staff of residential youth facilities.* Springfield, IL: Charles C Thomas.

Harris, J. R. Jr. (2003). *Respecting residential work with children.* Holyoke, MA: NEARI Press.

Laursen, E. K. (2004). Creating a change-oriented, strength based milieu. *Reclaiming Children and Youth, 13,* 16–21.

Maier, H. W. (1990). A developmental perspective for child and youth care work. In J. Anglin, C. J. Denholm, R. V. Ferguson, & A. R. Pence (Eds.), *Perspectives in professional child and youth care* (pp. 7–24). Binghamton, NY: Haworth Press.

Mayer, M. F. (1958). *A guide for child-care workers.* Washington, DC: Child Welfare League of America.

O'Halloran, T. M., & Linton, J. M. (2000). Stress on the job: Self care resources for counselors. *Journal of Mental Health Counseling, 22,* 354–364.

Siegel, D. J., & Hartzell, M. (2003). *Parenting from the inside out: How a deeper understanding can help you raise children who thrive.* New York: Jeremy P. Tarcher/Putnam.

Trieschman, A. E., Whittaker, J. K., & Brendtro, L. K. (1969). *The other 23 hours.* Hawthorne, NY: Aldine de Gruyter.

Whittaker, J. K. (1979). *Caring for troubled children: Residential treatment in a community context.* New York: Aldine de Gruyter.